The Abortion Debate
Understanding the Issues

ISSUES IN FOCUS TODAY

Johannah Haney

Enslow Publishers, Inc.
40 Industrial Road
Box 398
Berkeley Heights, NJ 07922
USA
http://www.enslow.com

Library of Congress Cataloging-in-Publication Data

Haney, Johannah.
    The abortion debate : understanding the issues / Johannah Haney.
        p. cm. — (Issues in focus today)
    Summary: "Examines the debate over abortion, discussing both the pro-life and pro-
        choice sides of the argument, the history and laws on abortion in the United States,
        and finding a middle ground on the issue"—Provided by publisher.
    Includes bibliographical references and index.
    ISBN-13: 978-0-7660-2916-3
    ISBN-10: 0-7660-2916-6
    1. Abortion—United States—Juvenile literature. 2. Abortion—Law and legislation—
United States—Juvenile literature. 3. Pro-choice movement—United States—Juvenile
literature. 4. Pro-life movement—United States—Juvenile literature. I. Title.
    HQ767.5.U5H356 2008
    362.198'8800973—dc22
                                2008013900

Printed in the United States of America

10 9 8 7 6 5 4 3 2 1

To Our Readers: We have done our best to make sure all Internet addresses in this book
were active and appropriate when we went to press. However, the author and the publisher
have no control over and assume no liability for the material available on those Internet sites
or on other Web sites they may link to. Any comments or suggestions can be sent by e-mail
to comments@enslow.com or to the address on the back cover.

♻ Enslow Publishers, Inc., is committed to printing our books on recycled paper. The paper
in every book contains 10% to 30% post-consumer waste (PCW). The cover board on the
outside of each book contains 100% PCW. Our goal is to do our part to help young people
and the environment too!

Illustration Credits: AJPhoto/Photo Researchers, Inc., p. 11; Anatomical Travelogue/Photo
Researchers, Inc., p. 49; AP/Wide World, pp. 3, 16, 25, 33, 36, 52, 56, 60, 65, 68, 72, 76,
85, 90, 97, 101; Reproduced from the *Dictionary of American Portraits*, published by Dover
Publications, Inc., in 1967, p. 29; Nicole DiMella, pp. 3, 44; Véronique Estiot/Photo
Researchers, Inc., p. 93; Getty Images, p. 1; Library of Congress, p. 39; Photos.com, pp. 3,
88; Shutterstock, pp. 3, 5, 20, 62, 79, 99, 103; Wikimedia Commons, p. 29 (left).

Cover Illustrations: Getty Images (large photo); BananaStock (small inset photo).

Chapter 1 Abortion: Opposing Viewpoints   5

Chapter 2 Abortion Throughout History   20

Chapter 3 The Pro-Choice Argument   44

Chapter 4 The Pro-Life Argument   62

Chapter 5 Opinions From the Middle Ground   79

Chapter 6 Abortion in the Twenty-first Century   90

Chapter Notes   96

Glossary   104

For More Information   106

Further Reading   107

Internet Addresses   108

Index   109

Abortion: Opposing Viewpoints

I have to get an abortion. *That was the very first thing that went through Lisa's mind when she looked down at the pregnancy test and saw the double lines that confirmed her worst fear. She was pregnant, nineteen, and scared. She says she felt like "someone being held under water . . . all you can do is struggle to find a way out. Abortion was the first thing that came to mind."*

Lisa didn't tell her parents, only her boyfriend. He drove her to an abortion clinic when she was eleven weeks pregnant. While they were driving in, people protesting at the clinic tried giving them literature through the car window. Lisa says, "All I saw were pictures of babies and I didn't want to see it. . . . I screamed to my boyfriend, 'Don't stop! Keep driving!'"

She says she remembers feeling numb while she filled out paperwork in the waiting room. The procedure itself was not long, Lisa remembers, but the time before while the staff prepares as well as the time after during recovery made the trip quite lengthy. "After the appointment I felt empty and alone," Lisa says.

Every woman reacts differently to the experience of abortion. For Lisa, her abortion caused her to become an active pro-life advocate. Today, she works to tell her story to other young women facing unplanned pregnancy.[1]

Lisa's story of unplanned pregnancy is not a unique one. In the United States, about half of all pregnancies are unplanned.[2] Of the abortions reported to the Centers for Disease Control and Prevention, about 82 percent are obtained by unmarried women, and 51 percent are obtained by women younger than twenty-five years old.[3]

What Is at Stake?

Women choose abortion for a variety of reasons. Some feel they are too young to be good mothers. Others fear that they will get

When Are Most Abortions Performed?

According to the Centers for Disease Control and Prevention, the vast majority of abortions—88 percent—are performed before thirteen weeks of pregnancy.

Percentage of abortions performed at:

8 weeks or fewer: 61%

9–10 weeks: 18%

11–12 weeks: 9.7%

13–15 weeks: 6.2%

16-20 weeks: 4.2%

21 weeks or more: 1.4%[4]

in trouble with their parents for having sexual intercourse or with their husbands for having an extramarital affair. Sometimes women feel having a baby is not the right thing at that time in their lives because they do not have enough money, are in school, are at a high point in their career, or already have children. When women are victims of rape or incest, many decide to abort the resulting pregnancies. With advanced medical testing, doctors can detect certain genetic illnesses at different points during pregnancy. Some women choose to end pregnancies in which the baby would have severe disabilities, and perhaps no real chance to live at all.

But some people think abortion should not be allowed in some, or even all, of these cases. They believe that the embryo or fetus is a life from the very beginning, and that life deserves to be protected from abortion, even if it is inconvenient for the mother. These people often characterize themselves as "pro-life." People who feel this way are often called pro-lifers.

People who believe women should have the right to decide whether they want to continue a pregnancy or end the pregnancy with an abortion usually refer to themselves as pro-choice. Pro-choicers believe women should have legal and safe access to abortion.

The debate between the pro-life side and the pro-choice side is intense and often emotional. Many people feel strongly that abortion should be either allowed or not allowed. The U.S. Senate and House of Representatives, as well as state governments, are all involved in the abortion debate when they decide what laws should govern abortion. The justice system has shaped the abortion issue dramatically when important court cases are decided, such as the landmark decision *Roe* v. *Wade*, which made abortion legal in 1973. Science shapes the abortion debate as advances in medicine allow doctors to detect problems in pregnancy better than ever before and as new techniques for abortions include easier, less expensive, and less invasive methods. This book will cover many different opinions about abortion as well as the history and politics of abortion, and it will examine how the abortion issue might change in the future.

Stages of Pregnancy

To understand the issues surrounding abortion, it is first necessary to know about pregnancy. When a man ejaculates during sexual intercourse, millions of sperm are released into the woman's vagina. The sperm swim through the vagina and past the cervix—the necklike opening to the uterus. Only a few hundred of the millions will make it to the fallopian tubes where, if the woman is ovulating, an egg, or ovum, is waiting. If a single sperm penetrates the egg, the egg is fertilized.

As soon as an egg is fertilized, the combination of the egg and sperm is called a *zygote*. The zygote begins to divide first into two cells, then four cells, then eight, and so on. Once it reaches between seventy and one hundred cells, the zygote is called a *blastocyst*.[5] The blastocyst continues to grow as it moves through the woman's fallopian tube into the uterus. About five days after fertilization, the blastocyst reaches the uterus and implants into the lining of the uterus. It is now called an *embryo*. Pregnancy does not actually begin until the blastocyst implants in the uterine wall and becomes an embryo.[6] Eight weeks after fertilization, the fetal stage begins. At this point, the term *fetus* is used instead of the term *embryo*.

Pregnancy is divided into three sections called trimesters. The first trimester lasts until the twelfth week of pregnancy. During the first trimester, the embryo (called a fetus after the eighth week) develops all the major structures of the body. The hands, feet, brain, heart, and organs are present by the eighth week of pregnancy, but they are still developing and growing. By the end of the first trimester, the fetus is about 3.2 inches long.[7]

The second trimester lasts from the thirteenth week until the twenty-fourth week. During the second trimester, the organs continue to develop. As muscles develop, the fetus begins moving more actively. At around the twentieth week of pregnancy, the mother can feel the fetus moving inside her. This is called quickening. At the end of the second trimester, the fetus is about 11.2 inches long and weighs 1 pound, 10 ounces.[8]

The third trimester starts at week twenty-five and ends upon delivery of the baby. In the first part of the third trimester, the brain and nervous system develop rapidly. The lungs also go through the last stages of development. Pregnancy is officially said to be forty weeks long, but a baby born at thirty-seven weeks is considered full term. During the third trimester, babies born prematurely, especially between weeks twenty-five and twenty-eight, are at high risk of severe complications or death. The longer the fetus remains in the womb, the better the outcome. (The most premature baby on record was born October 24, 2006. Baby Amillia spent just twenty-one weeks and six days in the womb.[9])

Some complications in pregnancy can lead to pregnancy loss, called a miscarriage. The medical term for a miscarriage is *spontaneous abortion*. It can happen any time in the first twenty weeks of a pregnancy, however, it is most likely during the first trimester. When a woman has a miscarriage, the embryo or fetus is expelled from her body, accompanied by bleeding, which can be heavy. No one knows for sure how many pregnancies end in miscarriage, because many miscarriages occur before the woman realizes she is pregnant. In the United States, about 15 percent of recognized pregnancies end in miscarriage, but medical experts say that as many as 50 percent of all pregnancies could end in miscarriage.[10] Usually a miscarriage occurs when there is a problem with the developing embryo or fetus, such as faulty chromosomes, which are the structures that carry genetic information. Hormonal problems in the pregnant woman can also cause miscarriage. Often the exact cause of a miscarriage is never known.

How Abortions Are Performed

There are two types of abortions used in the United States today: medication abortion and surgical abortion. Both require medical care and supervision and have their own advantages and risks.

Medication Abortion. Medication abortion can be performed in the earliest weeks of pregnancy, usually until the seventh week. It involves a pregnant woman's taking a combination of medicines that trigger the uterus to expel the embryo and pregnancy tissues. First, a woman takes a drug called mifepristone, known commonly as RU-486. Mifepristone makes the lining of the uterus get thinner and makes the cervix soft. Sometimes women are given methotrexate instead of mifepristone. Methotrexate is a drug that stops a pregnancy from developing further. It can also stop the growth of an ectopic pregnancy (a condition in which the embryo grows in the fallopian tube). This is important, because if an ectopic pregnancy continues to grow, it can cause the fallopian tube to rupture, which can be life threatening for the woman.

About two to three days after a woman takes mifepristone or methotrexate, she takes misoprostol, either by mouth or a dose placed inside the vagina. This drug causes strong contractions in the uterus that feel like severe menstrual cramps. As the uterus contracts, the embryo and tissue are forced out of the uterus.

A woman needs to see a doctor to find out if she is a good candidate for this method of abortion. If a woman and her health-care provider determine that a medication abortion is the best way to proceed, the patient is given the medications and instructions for using them. Usually the first drug, mifepristone, is given in the doctor's office. In some cases, the woman

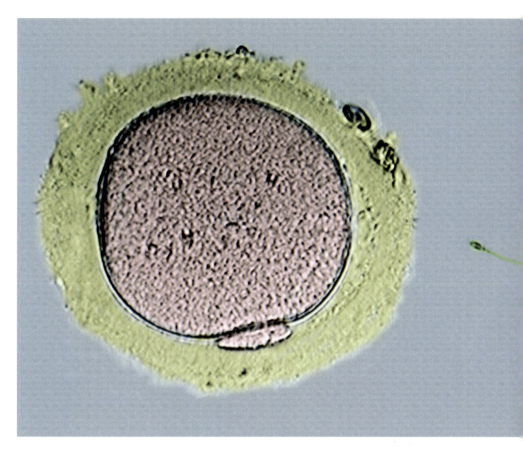

This microscopic image shows a sperm fertilizing an egg. Of the millions of sperm ejaculated, only a few hundred make it to the fallopian tube, and only one is able to fertilize the egg.

can then use the second drug, misoprostol, in the privacy of her own home. Several hours after taking misoprostol, a woman will start bleeding. It is usually heavier than a menstrual period. Side effects can include cramps, nausea, and diarrhea. After two weeks, the woman needs to have a follow-up appointment with her doctor for an ultrasound and blood tests to make sure the woman is healthy and that the abortion was completed.

Risks of medication abortion include hemorrhage— uncontrolled bleeding—and infection. For many women, having medication abortion feels similar to having a natural miscarriage. When medication abortion is carried out correctly, the success rate is 92 to 97 percent.[11] If a medication abortion fails to cause an abortion, a surgical abortion can be performed.

Surgical Abortion. Surgical abortion involves dilating the cervix (enlarging the opening of the uterus) and then removing the contents of the uterus. The cervix is the narrow lower portion of the uterus where it meets the vaginal canal. It has a small pinhole opening through which menstrual fluid flows out and sperm can travel in. In a surgical abortion, the cervix must be dilated to allow space for instruments to pass into the uterus. Surgical abortions are performed after six or seven weeks of pregnancy.

There are a few different ways doctors perform surgical abortions. All surgical abortions are performed in a clinic or doctor's office or, less often, in a hospital. Although they are called surgical abortions, women are usually not put under general anesthesia, which can pose added risks. Instead, women are given the option of which pain-reducing measures to use. Some choose to undergo sedation. Some clinics offer nitrous oxide (laughing gas) to help the patient relax. A local anesthetic can be given in the cervix to numb the area. The procedure usually requires a woman to be in the office for several hours so that the medical staff can perform blood testing before the procedure and can observe a woman for a period of time after the abortion to make sure there are no complications.

Abortion and Cancer

A lot of research has been done recently to determine the effects of abortion on women's health. Some studies have claimed that having a miscarriage or an abortion increases a woman's risk of breast cancer. In 2003, the National Cancer Institute studied the relationship and determined that miscarriage and abortion are not associated with a greater chance of developing breast cancer.[12]

One type of surgical abortion is suction aspiration. This procedure can be performed between six and twelve weeks of pregnancy. Patients undergoing suction aspiration are given a local anesthetic to numb the cervix. Then, cone-shaped rods are placed in the cervix to dilate it so that a cannula—a long flexible tube—can pass into the uterus. The cannula is attached to a suction device. When the suction is administered, the contents of the uterus pass through the cannula. The procedure itself takes about ten to twenty minutes. Many women feel cramping, nausea, and light-headedness after a suction aspiration. More serious complications include infection, heavy bleeding, and damage to the cervix or uterus, but these complications are rare.

Another method of surgical abortion is called dilation and curettage, often called a D&C for short. D&Cs can be performed between twelve and fifteen weeks of pregnancy. In this procedure, the cervix is dilated and a doctor uses a curette, which is a thin metal rod with a loop on the end, to scrape the lining of the uterus. D&Cs are also used in other medical procedures. Sometimes a woman needs a D&C to diagnose or treat gynecological problems when she is not pregnant. If a woman has a miscarriage, she may need a D&C to make sure all the contents of her uterus have been expelled. The side effects of a D&C might include bleeding, cramping, and nausea. Serious complications, such as perforation of the uterus, are rare.

Between fifteen and twenty-one weeks of pregnancy, dilation and evacuation, or D&E, can be performed. In a D&E, the abortion provider must insert laminaria into the cervix about twenty-four hours before the procedure. Laminaria is a type of kelp, and when sticks of dried laminaria are placed in the cervix, they absorb moisture and expand, thus dilating the cervix. On the day of the procedure, the cervix is further dilated using cone-shaped rods, as in a D&C, and suction aspiration. A cannula and a curette are used to remove the contents of the uterus. The procedure lasts about thirty minutes. D&Es are performed in hospitals more often than suction aspiration or D&Cs, because there is a greater risk of complications, such as bleeding, infections, or damage to internal organs.

Saline abortions, also called instillation abortions, involve injecting saline into the amniotic sac—the sac of fluid that surrounds the fetus. After the injection, the fetus stops developing and the woman begins to have contractions, which expel the fetus. However, this method is used rarely today.

Abortions performed after about twenty weeks of gestation are considered late-term abortions. There are three main ways to perform late-term abortions. One method is D&E. Another way is to induce early labor. In this method, medications are given that cause the uterus to begin to contract, much like it does in childbirth. The rhythmic contractions help move the fetus into the birth canal, and the woman pushes it out through her vagina. The third form of abortion used after twenty-one weeks of pregnancy is dilation and extraction (D&X). It is also known as intact D&E, or intrauterine cranial decompression. In a D&X abortion, laminaria are inserted into the cervix two days before the procedure. On the third day, the membranes that surround the fetus usually break and amniotic fluid that was surrounding the fetus rushes out (this is commonly known as the water breaking). When this happens, the patient returns to the hospital. The fetus is rotated within the uterus so the legs and arms can be brought into the vagina using forceps. A small cut is made at the base of the head of the fetus. A cannula is introduced, and the material inside the skull is suctioned out. Then, the rest of the fetus is brought through the vagina. This procedure is also commonly done in a hospital setting because the risk of complications is higher. Some D&X abortions are performed because there is a serious medical problem with the mother and continuing the pregnancy could put her health, or even her life, in danger. This is another reason a D&X abortion may be performed in a hospital.

Emergency Contraceptive Pills

Emergency contraceptive pills are a type of medication women can take to protect against pregnancy after unprotected sex, or if the contraceptive method failed—for example, if a condom broke during intercourse, allowing sperm to enter a woman's vagina. They are sometimes known as morning-after pills, but this term is not accurate, since they may be taken up to several days after intercourse, not necessarily the next morning.

These medications contain high levels of progestin, and some types also contain estrogen. Progestin is a hormone that can prevent fertilization of an egg or prevent a fertilized egg from implanting in the uterus. Estrogen prevents ovulation. Both progestin and estrogen are hormones that occur naturally in women. Pregnancy rarely occurs immediately after intercourse; sperm can live for a few days while they travel in search of an egg to fertilize. The pill can be taken up to seventy-two hours after intercourse, but the earlier it is taken, the higher the effectiveness.

The drugs are taken in two doses. The first dose is taken within seventy-two hours of unprotected sex. The second pill is taken twelve hours after the first pill was taken. However, emergency contraceptive pills are far less effective at preventing pregnancy than other forms of contraception. Treatment with Plan B, one type of emergency contraceptive pills, within

Viability

Many people would like to determine the exact point at which a fetus would be able to live outside the womb. If this point were indisputably identified, the question about when it is too late to have an abortion would be clear in the minds of many people. However, it is impossible to set an exact time that a fetus would be viable. Each pregnancy reaches viability at a different time, so there is no medical or legal way to define viability for all cases.

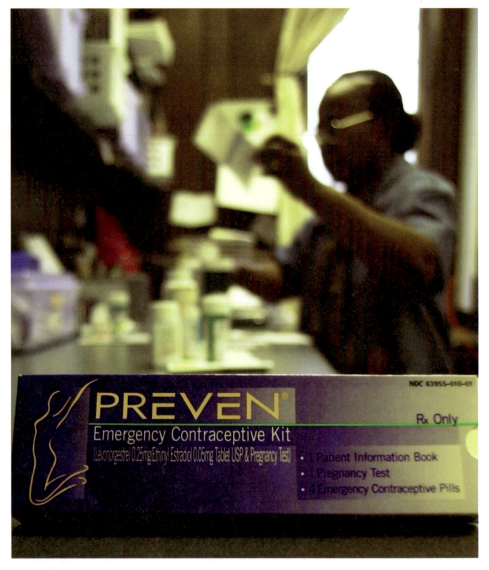

Emergency contraceptive pills, such as the Preven brand, prevent pregnancy with large doses of hormones. How they should be prescribed—or whether they should be available without prescription—is a controversial question.

seventy-two hours after one instance of unprotected sex reduces the risk of pregnancy by 89 percent.[13]

People disagree about whether emergency contraceptive pills are an abortifacient—something that induces an abortion. If a woman is already pregnant and she takes emergency contraceptive pills, the pills will not cause an abortion or miscarriage. Emergency contraceptive pills do not affect a pregnancy that already exists. But remember, by medical definition, pregnancy does not begin until after an embryo implants in the walls of a woman's uterus. So if a fertilized egg is still traveling to the uterus and a woman takes emergency contraceptive pills, the fertilized egg may not be able to implant in the wall of the uterus, and pregnancy will not occur. It is possible that a fertilized egg will fail to implant because of emergency contraceptive pills. This poses a moral obstacle for those who believe life begins at the moment of fertilization. But in strict medical terms, emergency contraceptive pills do not cause an abortion.

Opposing Viewpoints

The language surrounding the abortion controversy is very important in the political aspect of abortion. *Pro-choice* and *pro-life* are the terms that members of each of these groups prefer. Both sides use the positive prefix "pro" rather than the negative prefix "anti" to describe themselves. But sometimes, people from either side refer to the opposing group using the "anti" prefix. For example, pro-choicers might refer to pro-life activists as "anti-choice." Some pro-lifers refer to pro-choicers as "anti-life." Putting the opposing side in these negative terms is a politically charged way of manipulating the language of the abortion debate so their side seems more reasonable.

People who identify themselves as pro-choice believe in a woman's right to choose what is best for her. This does not mean, however, that someone who is pro-choice is pro-abortion and that abortion is preferred over childbirth. Most pro-choice advocates do not feel that way. Rather, they support a woman's right to choose whether to become a mother, to give up her baby for adoption, or to obtain an abortion.

In this book, we will use the terms that each side prefers when describing themselves: *pro-choice* and *pro-life*.

Other politically loaded terms involving abortions include:

- *Partial-birth abortion* vs. *D&X.* Many pro-lifers use the term "partial-birth abortion" for abortions performed by dilation and extraction. The term was coined by pro-life groups when laws banning the procedure were introduced in 1995.

- *Back-alley abortion* vs. *illegal abortion.* Pro-choicers often use the term "back-alley abortion" to refer to abortions that are performed illegally. This term is charged with graphic imagery, and neutral sources prefer simply "illegal abortion."

- *Embryo* or *fetus* vs. *baby.* Most pro-choicers use the terms "embryo," or "fetus" to describe the developing entity in pregnancy, and many pro-lifers use the term "baby." "Embryo" and "fetus" are medical terms with scientific definitions. "Baby" is not the correct medical term for a developing fetus, but the moral values regarding when

What Does *Pro-Life* Mean?

The term *pro-life* is most commonly understood in our culture to mean opposing abortion, but for some people, it also implies a certain viewpoint on other life issues, such as euthanasia and the death penalty. Some people who oppose abortion are in favor of a person's right to choose euthanasia, support capital punishment laws, or both. In this book, the term *pro-life* will refer to a person's position on abortion only, and it is not meant to assume people's views on other issues involving life.

life begins makes this the word of choice for many people who are pro-life.

- *Woman* vs. *mother.* Many pro-lifers refer to pregnant women as mothers regardless of whether the woman has other children or has an abortion. For pro-lifers, a woman becomes a mother from the moment an egg is fertilized, and she remains a mother even if she has an abortion and has no other children. Some pro-choicers see this as emotional manipulation.

Abortion is one of the most hotly debated issues today in the United States and abroad. The central issue in the debate revolves around the point at which a developing fetus becomes a person. No one thinks it is acceptable to terminate the life of a living person. But what people do not agree about is when the embryo or fetus becomes a living person on its own. People who identify with the pro-life ideology usually believe a new life exists from the moment of fertilization. In a Harris Poll, 88 percent of people who describe themselves as pro-life believe that life begins at the moment of fertilization.[14]

Pro-choicers usually view an embryo as a cluster of cells, not a person. But among people who identify themselves as pro-choice, not everyone agrees about when life begins. Fourteen percent of pro-choice advocates say life begins when the fetus has measurable brain activity or motion. Even among pro-choice advocates, 23 percent believe life begins at fertilization. Thirty-eight percent of pro-choice advocates believe life begins when the fetus would be able to survive outside the womb. Fifteen percent believe life begins at birth.[15]

Abortion was not always legal in the United States. Many factors aligned that brought the abortion issue to the forefront of political and moral debate in the past one hundred years—and even earlier.

Rue, an herb used to induce abortions in ancient times.

2 **Abortion Throughout History**

While abortion is one of the most hotly debated topics in modern times, it has been the subject of debate and scrutiny for thousands of years. The first evidence of abortion in history was in China around 500–515 B.C., where concubines to the royalty were given abortions if they became pregnant.[1] In some cultures in ancient Assyria, women who had abortions were impaled on a stake. There are written records from Pliny the Elder in A.D. 23 to 79 describing birth control methods and abortion techniques.[2] A Greek doctor from the first century writes that if a woman wants to end her pregnancy, "she should . . . leap energetically and carry things which are heavy beyond her strength."[3] Descriptions of using massage to stimulate abortion are well documented in parts of Asia since ancient times.

Throughout history, many different forms of abortion were performed. Certain herbs known to have abortifacient properties were administered orally or vaginally. Other methods of abortion described in historical documents involve putting pressure on a woman's uterus from outside, inserting long probes into the uterus, sitting in hot baths, and even trying to jump around to "shake" the fetus from the uterus.

Abortion and Religion

For some people, abortion is directly tied to their religious beliefs. Throughout history, many religions have changed their official views of abortion, sometimes based on advances in medical knowledge.

Other cultures allowed abortion before the woman could feel the fetus moving inside her, called quickening. This usually happens around the twentieth week of pregnancy, though women who have been pregnant previously may be able to sense quickening earlier.

Buddhism. Abortion is generally seen as an act of killing in the Buddhist religion. Buddhists believe a whole life exists from the moment of fertilization. However, there are different degrees of morality when it comes to abortion. If a woman had an abortion for purely self-serving reasons, the most severe amorality exists according to Buddhism. But if there are good intentions for having an abortion, such as preserving the life or health of the woman, or preventing suffering for a severely malformed fetus, the moral crime is not as severe. The Dalai Lama, the spiritual head of Tibetan Buddhists, says abortion "is an act of killing and is negative, generally speaking. But it depends on the circumstances. If the . . . birth will create serious problems for the parent, these are cases where there can be an exception.

I think abortion should be approved or disapproved according to each circumstance."[4]

Hinduism. The Hindu belief is that life—both physical and spiritual—begins from the moment of conception. For this reason, abortion is seen as one of the most terrible acts. However, if a woman's life is in danger or she risks grave injury by continuing with a pregnancy, more weight is given to the life of the mother, and an abortion may be performed. In the Hindu surgical guide *Susruta Samhita*, which dates back to the third or fourth century, abortions are recommended in cases where the fetus has a major defect.[5]

> Throughout history, many religions have changed their official views of abortion, sometimes based on advances in medical knowledge.

Islam. The Muslim religion prizes life. Historically, Muslim texts have asserted that the life of a fetus truly begins when it gains a soul, 120 days after fertilization. Different schools of Islam have different opinions about circumstances under which a woman can have an abortion before 120 days. The Zaydi school says women can seek an abortion before 120 days for any reason. Most Hanafi and Shafi'i scholars say a woman needs a good reason to have an abortion, such as a health risk to the woman. Some Maliki scholars strongly disapprove of abortion. The Zahiri, Ibadiyya, and Imamiyya schools forbid abortion at any time for any reason.[6] After 120 days, most scholars say abortion is allowed only to save the life of the pregnant woman. In general, Muslims value life and the potential for life and believe that the reasons for abortion must be compelling in order to justify it.

Judaism. Most forms of Judaism follow a moderate point of view on abortion. In Jewish law, babies do not become full people until the head emerges from the birth canal. Before that point, a fetus is a partial life. So, in cases where the life or health of a woman is at risk, Jewish law permits abortion.[7] For Reform Jews, individual circumstances play a major role in determining whether abortion is a moral choice in the Jewish faith, and a woman who is confronted with the issue is urged to seek counsel from a rabbi to help her make the right decision. Orthodox Jews have a more restrictive view on abortion, and they believe an abortion should not be performed except to save a woman's life. Conservative Jews also do not condone abortion except to save the mother's life, and also to preserve a mother's physical and emotional health, or if the fetus has a severe abnormality. In all forms of Judaism, abortion for convenience is not condoned. For example, a woman could not morally decide to have an abortion because it was not the right time in her life to have children.

Mormonism. The Church of Latter-Day Saints believes that abortion is one of the worst sins a person can commit. In fact, anyone who contributes to abortion by encouraging a woman to have an abortion, paying for an abortion, or performing an abortion is also subject to church discipline. However, if a woman's life is in danger, when a fetus has defects that will cause it to be stillborn, or when a pregnancy results from rape or incest, women may consult with church leaders to pray about whether abortion is the best action.

Protestant Christianity. The views of people of Protestant faiths vary widely. There are many different denominations of Protestant faith, and they have varying views on abortion. For example, the Presbyterian Church says a woman should have the option of choosing abortion at her own discretion, but that it should not be used as a method of birth control or gender selection, and that late-term abortions are "a matter of grave moral concern."[8] On the other hand, the Southern Baptist

Convention says: "At the moment of conception, a new being enters the universe, a human being, a being created in God's image. This human being deserves our protection, whatever the circumstances of conception."[9] Christian religions that are fundamentalist—that is, they believe a literal interpretation of the Bible is fundamental to leading a moral life—usually have very conservative views on abortion.

Roman Catholicism. The Catholic Church has held very strong beliefs about abortion over the centuries. In the fourth century A.D., St. Augustine said, "Abortion could be viewed as murder only if the fetus was judged a 'fully formed' human. [Forty] days for males and 80 days for females." This meant that abortion was not murder, but "a grave form of birth control." Early in the thirteenth century, Pope Innocent III said that abortion before quickening was not considered murder; before this point in pregnancy, abortion was still wrong, but a lesser sin. The greater sin, according to the Church, was adultery or promiscuous behavior that led to pregnancy in the first place. In the fifteenth century, St. Antonius, the archbishop of Florence, said that abortion should be permitted in early pregnancy to save the life of the pregnant woman.[10]

In 1588, Pope Sixtus V declared all abortion a sin, and he said a woman who had an abortion would be excommunicated, or excluded from church membership—the highest form of punishment in the Catholic Church. But just three years later, Pope Gregory XIV rescinded the law. Then, in 1869, Pope Pius IX once again put in place Pope Sixtus's rule: Abortion is a sin, regardless of when in pregnancy it is performed, and the penalty is excommunication.

Today, the Catholic Church doctrine states that abortion at any point is a sin. There is one situation in which most Catholic officials say abortion is permitted: if a woman has an ectopic pregnancy (the embryo is developing in the fallopian tube).

Pope Benedict XVI delivers a blessing in January 2008. The Roman Catholic Church's view of abortion has shifted somewhat over the centuries; today the Church holds that abortion at any point is a sin.

Religious Views

Many people who identify with a particular religion often look to the laws and history of their faith for cues to influence their personal views about abortion. But other people who are active in a particular religion disagree with their church's statements about the morality of abortion, and they form their own opinions about the issue. For that reason, it is impossible to determine what a person's beliefs about abortion are based only on which religion they practice.

Because the tube will rupture if left untreated, threatening the woman's life, surgical removal of the fallopian tube is allowed. In this case, the main intent is not to abort the fetus, though it is a known consequence. Although the embryo will certainly stop developing when it is removed in the fallopian tube from the woman's body, it is not the direct intent to abort the embryo.

However, the Church does not allow abortion in every case to save a woman's life. For example, if a woman has eclampsia, a condition that arises in pregnancy and can be fatal if the pregnancy continues, abortion is not allowed, even if the woman would die. And if a woman is diagnosed with liver cancer during pregnancy, it is not acceptable under church law for a woman to obtain an abortion so she can undergo chemotherapy or radiation treatments, which would cause severe harm to a developing fetus.

Abortion in the United States

When the first settlers came to the land we now call the United States, they followed the British Common Law. Since they came from the United Kingdom and had not yet set up their own rules for the land, they followed the same laws they used in their homeland. At this time, the Common Law said that abortion was allowed until quickening. So as long as a woman could not feel the fetus moving inside her, an abortion was legal. In fact, since there were no easy pregnancy tests, many women who stopped having a menstrual period sought treatment for "menstrual blockage" to allow a menstrual period to resume. This was essentially an abortion, but a woman may not have known for sure she was pregnant in the first place. After quickening, abortions were illegal.

In the 1800s and 1900s, advertisements in newspapers and magazines promised abortions through means of magic potions or pills. Many of these "potions" were simply poison. They could, indeed, cause an abortion, but many times they also caused the death of the woman. The risk to women's health was the motivation for America's first antiabortion regulations. In 1821, Connecticut passed a statue that said no woman could use dangerous poisons to try to cause an abortion.

The American Medical Association (AMA) launched a campaign in 1859 to make abortion illegal at any point in a pregnancy. One main motivation was the risk to women's health due to the methods of abortion at that time. Their campaign was successful. Within twenty years, more than forty laws restricting abortion were passed. These laws removed the difference between pre- and post-quickening so that abortion was illegal during the entire pregnancy. Many laws, however, allowed legal abortion if a woman's doctor believed it was necessary to save her life.

At this time, women desperate to have abortions found illegal methods. Some physicians were willing to perform illegal abortions, particularly for wealthy women who could afford to pay high prices. But many women who did not have the means to pay often risked their lives by getting dangerous abortions, either performed by illegal abortion providers, many of whom were not physicians and had no medical training, or by attempting to perform abortions on themselves.

In the late 1800s, women shared information on abortion techniques with one another. A physician from Chicago in 1900 said women would perform "violent exercise," jump off of chairs or roll down the stairs.[11] Women also took pills and drank teas thought to cause miscarriage, and they consulted midwives for advice about how to end a pregnancy. Some women tried using knitting needles or other long, sharp implements introduced into the uterus to try to cause miscarriages.

Most of these methods are unsafe, however, and many women died due to illegal abortions. The risk of infection was great because the instruments used were often not clean, and the environments in which illegal abortions usually took place were usually not sterile. Many people who performed illegal abortions were incompetent and caused serious damage, such as perforation of the uterus, bladder, or bowel.[12] Hemorrhage— or uncontrolled bleeding—was another very real threat. Complications such as this led to the hospitalization and death of many women who underwent illegal abortions.

Comstock Laws Force Abortion Information Underground.

Anthony Comstock was a man with a commitment to preventing anything obscene or offensive from being spread throughout the country. He jumped into the abortion debate with great vigor, making friends among legislators. He urged everyone he knew to support a ban on anything he considered to be obscene or pornographic, including information about birth control and abortion. In 1873, Comstock worked to promote the Act for the Suppression of Trade in, and Circulation of, Obscene Literature and Articles for Immoral Use, known as the Comstock Act. When it hit the desks of congressmen, no one wanted to speak against it because they feared others would think they supported obscenity.[13] The new law made it illegal to have or give to someone anything printed—including books, advertisements, pictures, and drawings—"for the prevention of

Anthony Comstock founded the New York Society for the Suppression of Vice in 1873. The organization opposed "improper" literature, including information about birth control.

contraception, or for causing unlawful abortion."[14] It was also illegal to distribute medications believed to induce abortion. Information on birth control and abortion were considered to be pornography. This meant that not only was it illegal to practice birth control and abortion—it was illegal even to discuss the subjects.

Although abortion was illegal in many cases during the late 1800s and much of the 1900s, law enforcement did not try to convict and punish every woman who obtained an illegal abortion. They did, however, prosecute people who performed abortions when the woman died due to complications.

Therapeutic Abortion. Some physicians were willing to help women obtain legal abortions by looking for reasons the pregnancy might endanger the woman's health. In states that allowed abortion to save the life of the woman—known as therapeutic abortion—some doctors would find or even invent risks in a pregnancy that would allow a woman to have an abortion legally. But doctors could face prosecution if they were discovered. In 1962, the American Law Institute drew up guidelines about criminal law to try to make laws more consistent from state to state. They called it the Model Penal Code. One area of the code was about how doctors could decide when a woman qualified for a legal therapeutic abortion. It stated that a doctor could perform an abortion if he or she believed that continuing the pregnancy would be detrimental to the woman's physical or emotional well-being, if the fetus had serious physical or mental defects, or if the pregnancy was the result of rape or incest. Some states adopted the guidelines in the Model Penal Code for their own state laws. So although most abortions were still illegal, there were some situations under which a woman could obtain a legal abortion in many states.

In the mid-twentieth century, several things happened to put the abortion laws in the United States under scrutiny. Rubella was one important factor in putting pressure on abortion laws. Rubella—or German measles—is a virus. It is mild in children and adults, causing low fever, headache, and an itchy rash. Some people with the disease do not even realize they have it because they do not feel very sick. However, if a woman is exposed to rubella in the early weeks of pregnancy, the fetus can develop a serious complication known as con- genital rubella syndrome. Babies born with congenital rubella syndrome display a range of physical and mental abnormalities, including heart defects, enlarged liver and spleen, eye disease, deafness, bone disease, seizures, and mental retardation.[15] Following the discovery of congenital rubella syndrome in the 1940s, some women who knew they had been exposed to rubella early in their pregnancies sought abortions because of the risk of the defects to their fetus.

The use of a drug called thalidomide in the late 1950s and 1960s also put abortion laws in question. Thalidomide is a tranquilizer developed in Europe, and one of its benefits is that it helps women suffering from morning sickness—nausea and vomiting often experienced during pregnancy, especially in the first trimester. Because of this, many pregnant women during this time were prescribed thalidomide in early pregnancy. But soon it became clear that the drug was causing severe abnormalities in the babies born to women who took the drug. Some of the babies had very short arms and legs, eye and ear defects, or malformed intestinal tracts.

Sherri Finkbine took the drug in 1962, and her doctor recommended an abortion due to the threat of fetal deformity. The case was surrounded by publicity and, as a result, the hospital in Arizona refused to treat her. The hospital was concerned about their criminal liability, since at the time, the state of Arizona allowed abortions only if the mother's life was threatened. Her doctor asked for a court order to proceed with the abortion, but it was denied. She began to get death threats, and the FBI was asked to protect her from harm. Sherri Finkbine and her husband went to Sweden, and she had a legal abortion there.

Many other things seemingly unrelated to abortion were happening in the United States in the 1950s and 1960s that led to abortion activism. The progression toward legalization of some abortions occurred during the women's rights movement. At a time when the country was energetically debating individual rights and freedoms, pro-choice activists claimed that abortion should be recognized as another "protected privacy right." Because of these social changes, the issue of abortion was directly related to women's independence.[16]

Legal Cases

A number of important legal cases led to changing laws about abortion.

Griswold v. Connecticut. In 1965, the case of *Griswold* v. *Connecticut* gave married couples the right to privacy within the boundaries of a marriage. Previously, contraceptives had been illegal in Connecticut. The Supreme Court decided that outlawing birth control intruded upon the lives of American couples and violated the constitutionally guaranteed right to privacy.[17] Although this law did not speak directly to abortion, it laid the foundation for future cases, and it was instrumental in the decision reached in the most groundbreaking abortion law in the United States, *Roe* v. *Wade.*

Roe v. Wade. Norma McCorvey, a twenty-one-year-old single woman living in Texas, was working as a ticket seller for a carnival in the summer of 1969. She had a five-year-old daughter who was being raised by McCorvey's mother and stepfather. When the summer ended, McCorvey lost her job and discovered she was pregnant. She wanted to end her pregnancy, but at that time in Texas, abortion was only allowed if it was necessary to save the woman's life. She was unable to find someone to perform the abortion illegally.

Meanwhile, Sarah Weddington, a young lawyer who herself had traveled to Mexico to get an abortion, was interested in putting together a court case to challenge the abortion laws at the time. Another lawyer introduced Weddington and McCorvey, and the beginnings of *Roe* v. *Wade* were under way with Weddington's colleague, Linda Coffee. (McCorvey used the pseudonym, or false name, of "Jane Roe" to protect her privacy, a practice that is common in legal cases. "Wade" was Henry Wade, the district attorney of Dallas County, who represented the state of Texas.)

Norma McCorvey used the pseudonym "Jane Roe" in the *Roe* v. *Wade* case that resulted in the liberalization of abortion laws nationwide. Later she became a pro-life activist.

The premise of the *Roe* v. *Wade* case resided on the issue that an abortion was a private matter that the federal government had no place interfering with. In 1973, the Supreme Court ruled that right to privacy included a woman's right to obtain an abortion if she did not want children. Seven justices voted in favor of Roe, and two justices (Byron White and William Rehnquist) voted against Roe. The ruling was largely based on the idea that a woman should be able to choose whether or not to bear children and that making such a decision should remain between a woman and her doctor.[18] The *Griswold* v. *Connecticut* case of 1965 was an important precedent for the *Roe* v. *Wade* ruling. Both cases cited the right to privacy as the reason for changing the laws. The law came too late for the lead plaintiff Norma McCorvey. She gave birth to a son and placed him for adoption. Later in her life, McCorvey became active in the pro-life movement.

Roe v. *Wade* liberalized the previous federal abortion law to allow women to have abortions for any reason up until the point in time when the fetus would be viable—around twenty-eight weeks. After that point, abortions would be allowed only in cases in which remaining pregnant would put the woman's life in serious jeopardy.[19]

After abortion was legalized on the federal level, states jumped in to enact their own laws in order to limit abortions within their jurisdiction. Many of these laws limited who was able to obtain an abortion; however, the federal government struck down many of these laws as they violated the precedents set in *Roe* v. *Wade*. In Missouri, women had to obtain their husbands' permission before getting an abortion until the law was overturned in 1976.[20] Also in 1976, Henry Hyde, a Republican congressman from Illinois, tacked on an amendment to the Department of Health, Education and Welfare appropriations bill—a law that says how the government can spend money—that banned funding from the federal government for abortions of any kind.[21]

Doe v. *Bolton.* Decided on the same day as *Roe* v. *Wade*, this case involved a young woman with the pseudonym of Mary Doe, who sued for the right to get an abortion in Georgia. Her lawyer, Margie Pitt Hames, filed the lawsuit against Arthur K. Bolton, the attorney general of Georgia. In a decision decided 7 to 2, the court found that doctors can consider every aspect of a woman's health, including "physical, emotional, psychological, familial and the woman's age" in deciding whether or not a woman should be permitted to have a legal abortion.[22]

Webster v. *Reproductive Health Services.* In 1986, Missouri lawmakers enacted a series of laws designed to reduce abortions. The preamble to the law stated that the "life of each human being begins at conception."[23] The laws themselves said that no public hospital or hospital worker could participate in performing an abortion, a doctor could not advise a woman to get an abortion, and doctors were required to test for viability after twenty weeks of pregnancy. A group of state employees and private healthcare providers that performed abortions sued the state, and the case made its way up to the Supreme Court. The Court was split in their decision of the case, but in 1989 decided that the state ban on abortion in state hospitals did not violate the Constitution. Since the preamble that defined life as beginning at conception was not applied in a way to specifically restrict abortion, it did not present a constitutional question.

Planned Parenthood v. *Casey.* In 1992, the Supreme Court took back some of the freedom the original *Roe* v. *Wade* decision provided, allowing states to create their own requirements about the circumstances under which women could get a legal abortion. The only stipulation is that these requirements cannot cause serious obstacles for a woman to obtain an abortion.[24] It also said a point of viability of a fetus could no longer be assumed as being as late as twenty-eight weeks. This took into account medical advancements since *Roe* v. *Wade* was first decided, though they did not put an exact time frame on the point of viability.[25]

Stenberg v. Carhart. After Nebraska outlawed late-term abortions without allowing for exceptions for the health of the mother, a case was brought to the Supreme Court arguing that physicians should be able to perform late-term abortions,

Dr. Leroy Carhart, a Nebraska gynecologist, went to the Supreme Court in an effort to uphold the legality of certain types of late-term abortions.

because banning them would place an "undue burden" on the mother—language taken from *Planned Parenthood* v. *Casey.*[26] The Court struck down the law, saying it violated the due process clause of the Constitution.

Trigger Laws and Protecting Abortion Rights

Trigger laws have been enacted by some states to ensure that abortion can be outlawed at the first possible opportunity. These laws state that abortion is banned, although some make exceptions if the life of the woman is at risk. However, these laws cannot be in effect unless *Roe* v. *Wade* is overturned by the Supreme Court. Mississippi, Illinois, Indiana, Kentucky, South Dakota, and Louisiana all have some form of trigger laws. Although the intent is that these states would automatically ban abortion if the Supreme Court overturned *Roe* v. *Wade*, legal experts disagree about whether these laws would actually be automatic, or if they would need to be activated by state's governor, attorney general, or lawmakers. Arkansas, Missouri, and North Dakota have made statements of policy, which means that if *Roe* v. *Wade* is overturned, they intend to ban abortion in their states. These statements of policy are not laws, however, and would not be effective immediately if federal laws on abortion changed.

Conversely, other states have passed laws that would ensure women still have access to abortion even if the federal laws governing abortion changed. These states include Hawaii, Nevada, Maryland, Maine, Washington, Connecticut, and California. In at least ten other states, the state's highest courts have "interpreted the state constitution as protecting a woman's right to abortion."[27] This means even if federal statutes changed, the state constitution would still guarantee a woman's right to choose abortion.

Politics and Abortion

Opinions on abortion oftentimes divide along political party lines. Traditionally, Republicans are pro-life and Democrats are pro-choice. However, as with religion, a person's political party does not tell the entire story of that person's feelings on abortion. A good example of this is the group Democrats for Life, a group of people who identify themselves as Democrats but are also pro-life. Republican Majority for Choice and Republicans for Choice are two organizations of Republicans who stray from their political party's pro-life stance, and, instead, they support reproductive freedom, including a woman's right to access abortion.

Each president who has been in office since the abortion debate heated up after *Roe* v. *Wade* has taken steps to have an impact on the face of abortion in the United States.

President Jimmy Carter. In 1976, Jimmy Carter was the Democratic nominee for president. He openly opposed abortion, directly contradicting his party's beliefs. He was on shaky ground with Democratic pro-choicers and agreed not to attempt to overturn *Roe* v. *Wade*. While he won the Southern vote, which consisted primarily of evangelical Christians, President Carter did not speak out against *Roe*. Sarah Wedding-ton—one of Carter's assistants—agreed to limit her requests for funding for abortion clinics.[28] This tumultuous "agreeing to disagree" did not bode well for either side of the issue.

President Ronald Reagan. President Reagan, a Republican and a staunch supporter of the pro-life movement, made considerable efforts during his presidency to overturn *Roe* v. *Wade* and to limit funding to abortion clinics. He is also responsible for the "withholding of U.S. foreign aid from international family planning agencies that promoted abortion."[29]

President Jimmy Carter (on left) was personally opposed to abortion, but he agreed not to try to overturn *Roe* v. *Wade*. Ronald Reagan, however, made concerted efforts to fight abortion during his presidency.

President George H. W. Bush. As vice president and then as president, George H. W. Bush worked to overturn *Roe* and to limit funding for abortion clinics. While he did support abortions in the cases of rape, incest, and serious health risk to the mother, he vetoed many bills that would have allowed federal funding for some cases of abortion.[30]

President Bill Clinton. President Clinton supported the decision made in 1973 by *Roe* v. *Wade* to legalize abortions and made many efforts to uphold it. He also appointed two pro-choice judges, Ruth Bader Ginsberg and Stephen Breyer, to the Supreme Court.[31] While he also strove to reduce abortions by encouraging adoption, he ultimately believed the decision to have an abortion remained a private matter and that a woman must "decide in consultation with her conscience, her doctor and her God."[32]

President George W. Bush. Always an advocate for pro-life policy, President Bush would like to limit abortions as much as possible. He signed the Partial Birth Abortion Ban Act of 2003 into law, which makes dilation and extraction abortions illegal.[33] He also limited the amount of money sent overseas to fund family-planning clinics that performed abortions. Even so, President Bush supports the use of abortion in the cases of rape and incest and if the mother's life is in danger.

State Restrictions

Ever since *Roe* v. *Wade*, states have been coming up with their own restrictions on abortion; some have been upheld, while others have been overturned. For instance, in Texas, a woman has to go through counseling and wait for a twenty-four-hour period before she can have an abortion. Some states also have a parental consent or notification laws that require young women under age eighteen to obtain parent consent or notify their parents before getting an abortion.

Partial-Birth Abortion Ban Act of 2003

The dilation and extraction method of abortion has been a recent topic of serious debate. Opponents call the D&X procedure "partial-birth" abortion because the lower extremities

Abortion Throughout the World

Two-thirds of the women in the world live in countries that offer some form of legal abortion. All Western European countries offer abortion for at least some reasons except for the Republic of Ireland, Northern Ireland, and Malta. Denmark was the first European country to offer abortion in the first trimester. Yet globally, seventy thousand women die each year as a result of complications from illegal abortions.[34] The World Health Organization estimates that of the forty to fifty million abortions performed throughout the world every year, half of them are under unsafe conditions.[35] In the following countries, abortion is either completely illegal or legal only in cases of rape, incest, or danger to a woman's life: Honduras, Colombia, Chile, Nicaragua, Peru, Venezuela, Ireland, Nigeria, Egypt, Iran, and the Philippines.

of a fetus are brought into the vagina before doctors collapse the skull and bring the fetus out whole. The first Supreme Court case involving late-term abortions was *Stenberg* v. *Carhart*, wherein a Nebraska law was struck down because it did not provide an exception for women whose lives were in danger. The Partial-Birth Abortion Ban Act of 2003 went to the Supreme Court and a decision was handed down on April 18, 2007, in *Gonzales* v. *Carhart*. The major debate was whether the law was unconstitutional because it did not include an exception for the health of the woman. In a 5 to 4 opinion, the Court upheld the law banning the method, saying "the Respondents have not demonstrated that the Act . . . imposes an undue burden on a woman's right to abortion based on its overbreadth or lack of a health exception."[36] The law went into effect for the first time after the ruling.

Justice Ruth Bader Ginsburg, the only woman on the bench, did not agree with her colleagues in the decision. She wrote:

Today's decision is alarming. . . . It tolerates, indeed applauds, federal intervention to ban nationwide a procedure found necessary and proper in certain cases by the American College of Obstetricians and Gynecologists (ACOG). . . . And, for the first time since *Roe*, the Court blesses a prohibition with no exception safeguarding a woman's health.[37]

Pro-choicers see the *Gonzales* v. *Carhart* decision as a major step backward for women's health and the strength of abortion laws in the United States. Pro-lifers celebrate the decision as a step forward in protecting the lives of the unborn and toward dismantling *Roe* v. *Wade*.

Clinic Violence and Freedom of Access

In the 1990s, pro-life activists were protesting at clinics with increasing frequency, and sometimes with violence. According to the National Abortion Federation, there have been 5,672 instances of clinic violence in U.S. history.[38] The goal of many of these violent protests was to prevent abortion providers, clinic staff, and patients from being able to get inside the clinic. In 1994, the Freedom of Access to Clinic Entrances Act was passed. This law prohibits using intimidation, physical force, or barricades to prevent or discourage people from entering clinics. The law also specifies penalties for destruction of clinic property.

Precautions Against Violence

Many abortion providers work in a community outside of the one in which they live for safety reasons. Dr. John Smith, however, lives and works in the same community. In order to avoid potential violence and preserve anonymity in his community, he drives to a predetermined spot that changes regularly, where he is met by a police escort, which brings him to work. Dr. Smith wears a costume to work so protesters will not be able to recognize him in the community.[39] He asked that his name and identifying characteristics be changed for this book to protect his anonymity.

Opposing Viewpoints

The abortion debate goes beyond court battles and political strategy. Abortion is an issue that affects women and families in a most profound and intimate way. For those who strongly oppose abortion or fight passionately for abortion rights, the issue means far more than what this book has discussed so far.

3   The Pro-Choice Argument

When Olivia was seventeen, she missed her period. A home pregnancy test indicated she was pregnant. Olivia was on her high school track team, worked twenty hours a week, and maintained high grades in honors classes. She writes: "I couldn't even conceive of having a child then; of being a pregnant high schooler; of letting my family down; of the shame I would feel if anyone else knew; of not going to college. There were so many reasons to have the abortion, in my mind, and virtually no reasons not to have one."

Olivia only told her boyfriend, who was six years older than she, about the pregnancy. She decided very quickly that abortion was the best option for her. She called a local Planned

Parenthood clinic and made an appointment. Getting the abortion was difficult for Olivia. She didn't have a lot of money, so she chose the least expensive option, which involved very little anesthesia. She says the procedure was painful for her, but the nurse was very supportive and helped Olivia through the procedure, a kindness she still appreciates today. Olivia is now studying medicine; she writes: "I want to especially provide other women with the same level of compassion and non-judgment that that nurse provided to me."

Olivia does not regret her decision to have an abortion. "I look back on the experience and thank goodness that I had the legal right to seek an abortion. I was so young at the time, that I really do feel I made the right decision," she says. But she will never forget her experience with abortion. "I try to let it motivate me to help others, so that that tiny life that was beginning inside of me will continue to teach me for the rest of my life; so it will motivate me to be the best person I can be and to help others do the same for themselves."[1]

Some of the basic beliefs of people who are pro-choice can be summed up as follows:

- It is a woman's right to decide about her own fertility.

- The government should not make laws telling women what they can do with their bodies.

- Outlawing abortion would make women turn to illegal and unsafe methods to end their pregnancies.

- Unwanted children are more likely to be abused.

- Abortion helps prevent overpopulation.

- A woman's rights are more important than those of a fetus.

- Abortion is safer than childbirth at every stage.

- Abortion should be safe and accessible to any women who wants or needs one.

These beliefs affect people's positions on various areas of the abortion controversy, such as access to abortion and birth control, sex education, and crisis pregnancy centers. This chapter will explore some of these issues from the pro-choice side of the fence.

Access to Abortion

A major issue for pro-choicers is broadening women's access to abortion. Although *Roe* v. *Wade* made abortion legal, it is not always easy for a woman to find an abortion provider near her home or work. Clinic protests and violence can make it difficult for women to get into clinics. The costs of abortion are significant, which can be especially difficult for poor women. Laws that place obstacles to women getting abortion are also a cause pro-choicers typically rally against.

Pro-choice organizations such as the National Abortion Federation, Planned Parenthood Federation of America, NARAL Pro-Choice America, and others strive to make abortion easier for women to obtain. As of early 2007, 88 percent of counties in the Unites States did not have an identifiable abortion provider.[2] The majority of abortion providers are located in urban areas, so women who live in rural areas often must travel fifty miles or more to receive an abortion.

Reproductive Health Centers

Reproductive health centers, such as Planned Parenthood Federation of America, provide free or low-cost sexual health services to men and women of all ages. The full-spectrum of reproductive health services are provided, including birth control, emergency contraception, abortion, screening for sexually transmitted disease, screening for certain kinds of cancer, counseling and more. Reproductive health centers are often funded by donations, fees for services, and government grants. Planned Parenthood, the largest reproductive health center in the United States, received $305.1 million in government grants from June 2005 through June 2006.[3]

One reason abortion providers are hard to come by is that some states have laws that say only doctors can perform abortions, even though physician assistants are trained and qualified to provide abortion services. Exacerbating the problem is the fact that fewer doctors than in the past are learning to perform abortions, because some people are not interested in learning, and because teaching programs do not offer training as often as before.[4] Many abortion providers are reaching retirement age, and not as many doctors are being trained to replace them. Fewer abortions are being performed in hospitals, where medical students and interns train and learn new procedures, than in other settings like doctors' offices or clinics. Because of this, fewer new doctors have experience performing abortions. According to Medical Students for Choice, a nonprofit group that advocates teaching abortion procedures to medical students, many of today's younger doctors lack commitment to safe abortion because they "have not been faced with the spectre of unsafe abortion."[5] Young doctors also see doctors who do perform abortions being harassed or threatened with bodily harm. Medical Students for Choice are working to make sure more physicians are able to perform abortions, especially emergency procedures like D&Cs for patients who need immediate care, and so that doctors can advise their patients on the range of options available to them when faced with an unplanned pregnancy.

> A major issue for pro-choicers is broadening women's access to abortion. It is not always easy for a woman to find an abortion provider close by.

Parental Consent and Notification. Other obstacles make obtaining an abortion difficult for women. One is parental notification or consent laws. States with parental consent laws require that young women under a certain age (eighteen in most states with this law) obtain permission from one parent before an abortion provider is legally allowed to perform the procedure. Other states require that parents be informed of the minor's decision to obtain an abortion; however, the parent need not give his or her permission. If a pregnant teen fears violence from her parents, or if the pregnancy is the result of incest, she can apply for a judicial bypass. This means that she may be given permission by a judge to obtain an abortion without the knowledge of her parents. The exact process varies from state to state, but a young woman may file a petition with the circuit court. A woman may bring her own lawyer, or an attorney will be appointed for her for free. A private hearing is set within forty-eight hours of the application, in which the judge, the young woman, and her attorney are present. In general, judges want to see a young woman demonstrate that she is mature enough to make the decision to have an abortion without input from her parents. The judge also expects to hear why the young woman does not feel she can inform her parents of her pregnancy or decision to abort, for example, if she fears emotional or physical harm, or if the pregnancy was the result of sexual assault by a family member. In cases where pregnancy occurs from sexual violence or assault, whether by a family member or anyone else, the judge is required to file a police report. In most states, judicial bypass proceedings are confidential, except if sexual violence is involved. The judge typically informs the young woman of his or her decision at the hearing, but the judge has up to five days to make the decision. If the judicial bypass request is denied, a woman can appeal to higher courts, which must respond within ten days.

Counseling and Waiting Periods. Some states mandate that a woman who seeks an abortion must be counseled about abortion—sometimes in person—then wait for some period of time before undergoing the procedure. The state often provides the information an abortion provider must give the woman during counseling, and it often includes information about stages of fetal development, risks associated with abortion, and alternatives to abortion. The amount of time a woman must wait after receiving this material varies from one state to another and ranges from one hour to three days. The idea is that a woman must wait a period of time to reconsider whether she wants to receive an abortion.

Pro-choice advocates believe these laws put women's health at risk. The longer a woman must wait to obtain an abortion, the more risks to the woman's health. Abortion procedures get more complex as pregnancy progresses. According to Dr. John Smith, an abortion provider in the Midwest, this requirement can lead to more significant delays than just a day or two.

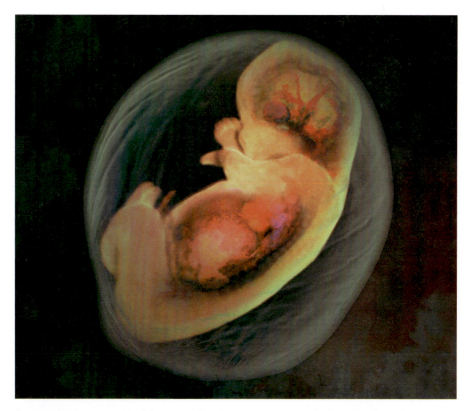

A computer-generated image of a fetus at ten weeks' gestation. Some states require that women seeking abortion be given information about fetal development.

He explains that in some states, there are so few abortion providers that a doctor flies in from out of town one day per week to provide services to women in an area. If she is required to receive counseling at the doctor's office or clinic and then wait a set length of time, the earliest she could legally get an abortion would be one week later, when the doctor returned to her area.[6] Because the waiting period laws require two visits to the doctor's office or clinic—one to receive the information and one to return after the waiting period for the procedure—the costs of abortion rise, limiting access to poor women and women who do not live near an abortion provider.

Cost of Abortion. The costs associated with abortion can make it difficult for a woman to obtain the procedure. The costs of abortion vary greatly depending on the stage of pregnancy, the abortion laws in her area, and what form of anesthesia the woman chooses. The typical cost is between three hundred and six hundred dollars for a first-trimester abortion to several thousands of dollars for abortions performed later in pregnancy, performed in a hospital, or for women with other medical conditions. Factors such as time missed from work and child care contribute to the cost of abortion.

Abortion Laws, State-by-State

States that enforce parent consent laws[7]
AL, AZ, AK, IA, IN, KS, KY, LA, ME, MA, MI, MS, MO, NC, ND, NE, OH, PA, RI, SC, SD, TN, TX, UT, VA, WI, WY

States that enforce parental notification laws[8]
CO, DE, FL, GA, IA, KS, MD, MN, NE, OK, SD, UT, WV

States that require a waiting period[9]
AL, AK, GA, ID, IN, KS, KY, LA, MI, MN, MS, MO, NB, ND, OH, OK, PA, SC, SD, TX, UT, VA, WV, WI

States that require counseling sessions[10]
AK, IN, LA, MS, OH, UT, WI

One reason pro-choicers usually oppose mandatory waiting periods is that it adds to a woman's cost for abortion. If a woman must make two visits to her doctor's office or clinic, she must pay fees for each visit in addition to the cost of missing work or paying for child care. They also believe these laws imply that a woman does not know what she is doing or that she does not truly know what she wants.

Some health insurance plans cover some portion of the fees for an abortion. Federal programs that provide health-care coverage for low-income people, such as Medicaid, do not cover any of the costs of abortion, however. Pro-choicers would like that to change. In 1976, Congress passed the Hyde Amendment, which says that federal funds will not be used for abortion, except in cases of rape or incest, or if the pregnancy puts the woman's life in danger. This prohibition includes, in addition to women on Medicaid, those on federal insurance plans, such as federal employees, Peace Corps volunteers, American Indians, federal prisoners, and members of the military. Pro-choicers want the Hyde Amendment to be repealed so that more women have access to abortion.

Birth Control

Although birth control is not abortion, people who are pro-choice often support easy and affordable access to birth control, such as birth control pills; emergency contraceptive pills; intrauterine devices (IUDs); Depo-Provera (a hormonal birth-control method given by injection every three months); condoms, diaphragms, and other barrier methods; spermicidal gels; and surgical sterilization—a permanent form of birth control in which the fallopian tubes are severed so that no eggs can come in contact with sperm.

Most women can obtain a safe form of birth control either by prescription from their doctors (birth control pills or emergency contraceptive pills) or simply over-the-counter (for

A nurse shows some of the contraceptives dispensed at a Planned Parenthood clinic. Pro-choicers support affordable access to birth control methods.

example, condoms and spermicidal jelly). However, some women cannot afford regular visits to a doctor or prescription medication; others cannot afford nonprescription methods. Some are under the age of eighteen and are afraid their family doctors will tell their parents that they asked about birth control.

Another obstacle to birth control that pro-choicers address is the ability for a woman to fill her prescription for oral contraceptives or emergency contraceptive pills at any pharmacy. Currently, pharmacists in some states who do not wish to fill a legal prescription for hormonal birth control or emergency contraception are free to refuse. Some pharmacists have even refused to return a woman's prescription slip so that she will not be able to fill the prescription at another pharmacy. Pharmacists can refuse to fill a legal prescription for oral contraceptives even if a woman is taking the pill for a medical reason other than birth control, such as treating fibroids or severe menstrual cramps. Pro-choice advocates believe that women should be able to fill their legal prescriptions at any pharmacy and that all pharmacists should fill prescriptions for oral contraceptives and emergency contraceptive pills regardless of their personal beliefs. In 2005, the Access to Legal Pharmaceuticals Act was introduced in the House of Representatives and the Senate. This bill would guarantee access to oral contraceptives at all pharmacies. According to the bill, if a pharmacist has a personal objection to filling a prescription for oral contraceptives, the pharmacy is required to make sure another pharmacist who does not object fills the prescription promptly.[11] Pro-choicers are still working to try to make this a law in the United States.

Pro-choicers also usually advocate federal legislation to ensure insurance coverage for prescription birth-control methods. Health insurance coverage usually covers most prescription medication, but not all health insurance plans cover birth-control prescriptions such as oral contraception.

Birth Control Pills: Can They Cause Abortions?

The reason some pro-life pharmacists refuse to fill prescriptions for oral contraceptives is because they say that in some cases, oral contraceptives can cause abortions. The birth control pill is designed to prevent ovulation. If no ovulation takes place, there is nothing to be fertilized by sperm. But in rare cases, usually when the pill is taken incorrectly, ovulation takes place anyway. If the pill fails to prevent ovulation and an egg is fertilized, some doctors have said the hormonally altered lining of the uterus might not be able to support implantation of the fertilized egg. However, scientists and doctors have not been able to agree if this effect takes place. Even the American Association of Pro-Life Obstetricians and Gynecologists acknowledges that no one knows for sure if oral contraceptives can cause a fertilized egg to fail to implant.[12]

As of early 2007, twenty-six states ensure that health insurance plans that offer prescription drug coverage also cover prescription contraceptives to the same extent as other medication.[13]

Sex Education

Sex education is a means of informing young people about sexual health issues, including pregnancy, sexually transmitted diseases, sex, and relationships. The stance on what should or should not be taught in school is a hotly debated issue.

People in the pro-choice camp are usually advocates of sex education in schools and at home. But they advocate a certain kind of sex education. They believe that sex education must be comprehensive and age appropriate, and it should include discussions of sexual intercourse, sexually transmitted diseases, methods of birth control, healthy sexuality, date rape and other forms of sexual violence, body image, the influence of drugs and alcohol on sexual activity, pregnancy, childbirth, and parenting. This approach is called comprehensive sex education. Some pro-choicers also call it medically accurate sex education.

Pro-choicers advocate comprehensive sex education in response to schools that use an abstinence-only approach to sex education. In this form of sex education, teachers emphasize that abstinence—or refraining from sex—is the only way to prevent pregnancy and sexually transmitted diseases. When methods of contraception and protection from STDs are mentioned at all, their failure rate is the main focus. Students do not usually learn about how to protect themselves from pregnancy and sexually transmitted diseases if they do become sexually active. The Social Security Act of 1996 outlines the criteria a program must meet to qualify as abstinence-only sex education. It says that an abstinence-only sex education program must teach exclusively the social, psychological, and health benefits of abstinence, that abstinence is the expected standard for unmarried adolescents, that abstinence is the only certain way to avoid pregnancy and sexually transmitted diseases, and the importance of reaching self-sufficiency before engaging in sexual intercourse.[14]

There are no reliable statistics about the number of schools that teach abstinence-only sex education, but the federal government proposes $204 million to fund abstinence education for adolescents in the year 2008.[15] People who advocate for comprehensive sex education believe the government should not fund abstinence-only sex education.

Comprehensive sex education can also include abstinence as one of the topics students learn about. But this method also includes information about other means of contraception, as well as other ways to protect against sexually transmitted disease. Olivia, who was mentioned at the beginning of this chapter, writes: "It's only now that I've entered medical school that I feel I am getting a comprehensive education on STDs, and it was only in college that I felt I was first properly introduced to birth control."[16]

Proponents of comprehensive sex education believe that young adults should have access to this information earlier. They believe that it is unrealistic to expect all teens to remain abstinent until marriage, and that when teens do engage in sexual activity, they are unprepared for ways to protect themselves from unwanted pregnancy and disease. A government-sponsored study showed that teens who participated in one of the tested abstinence-only education programs did not wait longer than teens in a control group before having sex. These teens also were more likely to believe that condoms are never effective at preventing STDs.[17]

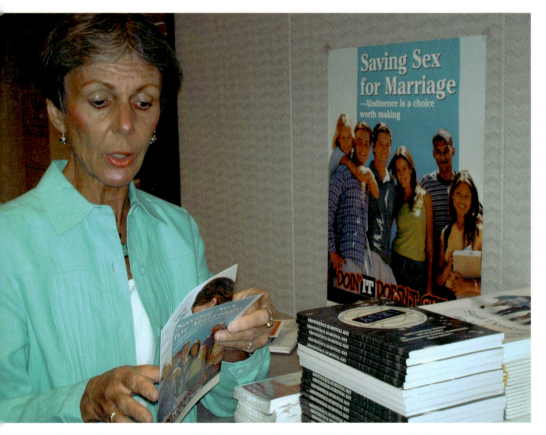

Susan Stewart directs the Alabama state health department's Abstinence-Until-Marriage Education Program. Supporters of comprehensive sex education argue that the government should not fund abstinence-only programs.

About 54 percent of women who have an abortion say they used some method of birth control in the month they became pregnant; but only 13 percent of women who were using the birth control pill and 14 percent of those using condoms say they used the method correctly.[18] Pro-choicers envision a world in which all students learn the facts about how using methods of contraception can reduce the number of unplanned pregnancies, which would drastically reduce the number of abortions.

Legal Advocacy

Pro-choice organizations such as NARAL Pro-Choice America, Planned Parenthood, and others have additional issues that they aim to educate people about and lobby for as well. These issues do not necessarily deal directly with abortion, but they are part of their mission so that abortion rights are protected and that women have the opportunity to prevent abortion by being given the education and means of birth control. This section will highlight a few of these issues.

One issue pro-choice organizations fight for is more comprehensive health-care coverage for birth control. In March 2007, for example, the U.S. Court of Appeals for the Eighth Circuit ruled on a case against Union Pacific Railroad about health insurance coverage for birth control pills. The plaintiff accused the railroad of having a policy of discriminating against women because the health insurance plan covered medications like Viagra and Rogaine for men but did not cover prescription contraceptives for women. In this case, the appeals court upheld the lower court's ruling that the railroad did not discriminate against women, because the health-care plan did not provide contraceptive coverage for men either. One of the judges, U.S. Judge Kermit Bye, did not agree, however. He wrote in his opinion:

> This failure only medically affects females, as they bear all of the health consequences of unplanned pregnancies. An insurance

policy providing comprehensive coverage for preventative medical care, including coverage for preventative prescription drugs used exclusively by males, but fails to cover prescription contraception used exclusively by females, can hardly be called equal. It just isn't so.[19]

The women who filed the lawsuit hope that the issue will be taken up by Congress to make companies that provide health insurance for preventative care to cover prescription contraceptives under the plan.

Crisis Pregnancy Centers

Crisis pregnancy centers (CPCs), also called pregnancy resource centers, are nonprofit organizations run by pro-life advocates. They offer women a place to go when faced with an unexpected pregnancy. Women can receive free services at these centers, including pregnancy tests, HIV tests, ultrasounds, and counseling. They also help women get the social services they may need, such as job training, housing, or government assistance. A defining characteristic of crisis pregnancy centers is that they do not offer abortion and often do not offer birth control. These centers are often funded by church groups and pro-life individuals. Some federal funding is given to help some centers operate. Since 2001, more than $30 million in federal money has gone to crisis pregnancy centers.[20]

Pro-choice activists campaign against crisis pregnancy centers run by pro-life activists. Often these centers actively try to dissuade women from considering abortion. Some provide ultrasounds to pregnant women, which show the developing fetus, though the staff members at pregnancy resource centers rarely have any medical training. Pro-choicers charge that these ultrasounds are a way of manipulating women into continuing their pregnancies.

Pregnancy resource centers often provide assistance to women who feel they cannot afford to have a child. They might provide maternity clothes, baby clothes and furniture, and even help buying food. People who oppose pregnancy resource centers say that this help is short-sighted, and that the help they give is short-lived. What happens to mothers when the pregnancy resource center is no longer helping them, but the bills are piling up? they ask.

Pro-choicers feel many of these centers are deceptive in their methods. Planned Parenthood, a pro-choice organization that opposes crisis pregnancy centers, says:

> CPCs pose as objective health facilities using neutral-sounding names and deceptive advertising practices that lead women facing unintended pregnancies to believe that they will be offered unbiased counseling and a full range of reproductive health services. Unsuspecting women are lured into [pregnancy resource centers] with the offer of free pregnancy testing or HIV tests.[21]

On March 30, 2006, Representative Carolyn Maloney, a Democrat from New York, introduced the Stop Deceptive Advertising for Women's Services Act into Congress. This bill prohibits pregnancy resource centers from advertising that they provide abortion services if they actually do not. This would require pregnancy resource centers to be more up front about the services they provide. In July 2006, Democratic Representative Henry Waxman of California prepared a congressional report on pregnancy resource centers that were receiving federal funding. The report found that 87 percent of the pregnancy resource centers polled gave women misleading and sometimes flat-out wrong information about the health effects of abortion—for example, that an abortion increases the risk for breast cancer, that abortion has a major impact on the ability to have children later, or that abortion leads to mental illness.[22] These members of Congress do not believe federal money should go to programs that are providing false information in order to serve a pro-life agenda.

A central part of the pro-choice argument is that a woman should be able to decide for herself whether or not to have a baby.

The Future of the Pro-Choice Advocates

Pro-choice organizations and activists will continue to support legislation that contributes to freedom of choice for abortion and work to make new laws that promote the pro-choice viewpoint. They continue to promote easier access to abortion and general health care for women, including access to birth control and other women's health services. The true motive for many pro-choicers is to protect women from the consequences of illegal or inaccessible abortion. Dr. John Smith, an abortion provider working in the United States, imagines what would happen if abortion were outlawed or made so restrictive that many women could not obtain legal abortions:

> Abortion bans would really affect women's health adversely. Women would continue to get abortions, legal or not. People with money would travel, or find a complicit physician to find a way to say that their health (usually mental health . . .) is at risk. Medication-initiated abortions would become the norm for others. . . . Women [would] obtain misoprostol on the Internet. . . . The darker side of this is that illegal abortion clinics would evolve. Hopefully they would be safer than they have been in the past. People without access to Internet or other means would use these clinics. We would find ourselves back in the 60s with septic complications and perforated uteruses.[23]

Alexander Sanger, the grandson of Margaret Sanger, an advocate for birth control from the 1910s to 1960s, writes: "We should continue to make our traditional arguments because they do persuade our core supporters. But a new framework is needed in order to bring along the 50 percent of the public that is nominally pro-choice but which may believe abortion immoral and accepts restrictions on abortion access."[24]

4   The Pro-Life Argument

Rachel had just started her sophomore year of high school. She had the same boyfriend for almost a year and lots of friends, she earned good grades in school, and she was active in school committees. That fall, she realized she might be pregnant. She tried not to think about it, but everywhere she went she saw pregnant women and babies and she was forced to confront the issue.

Rachel told her mother when she started having sex and her mom was the one to buy a pregnancy test for her. The test was positive and was confirmed by a doctor. Rachel says she felt ashamed and stupid that she had let everyone down. Rachel's boyfriend was angry at first—he threw a soda bottle and began yelling expletives.

After a few minutes he calmed down and told Rachel he loved her and that everything would be okay. But Rachel was not convinced.

She got advice from lots of people. Her doctor gave her information about adoption. Her school nurse gave her information about abortion and she considered it, thinking that if she got an abortion, maybe things could just go back to the way they were before.

But she knew that no matter which direction she chose, things would never be exactly as they had been. Although Rachel's father was angry at first, he eventually was able to get past his disappointment and be supportive of her. Rachel's mom and grandparents were also there for her. Because she felt like she had a strong system of support, Rachel decided she could have her baby and raise her with the help of the people around her. During her sophomore year, Rachel dropped out of high school and she received her GED before her daughter was born. Just two months after she had her daughter, Rachel started taking classes at the local university.

Life as a teen mother was not easy, and Rachel's life changed dramatically. "I didn't spend every weekend with my friends going to different parties, and hanging out," she says. "I didn't spend hours getting my makeup to look just perfect, or making sure my hair was just right. I didn't sleep in on Saturday mornings, and I didn't stay out all night on Friday night." Rachel and the father of the baby are not together anymore, but he continues to see the baby about every other weekend.

Now, Rachel is twenty and she just got married. She is in her third year of college studying speech communication and psychology. She works part-time and plans to go to graduate school. Rachel says, "Being a mother is so much work, but it is such a rewarding job . . . people have supported me so much more than I imagined they would."[1]

People who are pro-life believe that abortion is taking the life of a separate human being. Other key beliefs of most pro-lifers can be summed up as follows:

- A human being exists from the moment of conception.

- A fetus deserves the same rights as any other person.

- Abortion is against God's law.

- Abortion hurts women, emotionally and physically.

- Abortion devalues all life.

- No one needs an abortion, since there are families willing to adopt.

- Abortion should not be legal.

Pro-lifers work to overturn *Roe* v. *Wade* and other laws that make abortion legal. At the same time, many pro-life organizations recognize that women who face unplanned pregnancy—particularly young women under the age of eighteen—need help, and they offer assistance in the form of financial and emotional support.

This chapter will explore various issues related to the abortion controversy from the pro-life viewpoint.

Crisis Pregnancy Centers

Pro-life crisis pregnancy centers, also called pregnancy resource centers, reach out to women who are facing unplanned pregnancy and help them find alternatives to abortion through either adoption or choosing parenthood. These centers offer their clients a variety of practical services, including free pregnancy tests, ultrasound, and testing for sexually transmitted diseases; maternity clothes, baby clothes and other equipment such as cribs, diapers, and baby formula; referrals for medical care, counseling, legal assistance, job training and housing; help navigating paperwork to sign up for government assistance, if necessary, such as Medicaid and food stamps; and sometimes even cash to use for expenses related to pregnancy or child care.

Pregnancy centers offer a range of spiritual and emotional support as well. They know that women who are facing unplanned pregnancy are often scared and need help getting

Women and children at the North Side Life Care Center in Minneapolis. Like other crisis pregnancy centers, this one offers support to low-income women and tries to persuade them to have babies rather than abortions.

perspective on the situation. Some centers also help women make a plan for telling family or significant others about the pregnancy.

Another service many pregnancy resource centers provide is support for women who have had an abortion and are suffering psychological consequences. Pregnancy resource centers offer assistance to women who are experiencing what they call postabortion syndrome. They may counsel women at their own center or make referrals to mental health professionals in the community. There are hotlines available for women who have had abortions that provide information, resources, and support.

Among the pro-life community, there are different approaches to how a pregnancy resource center is operated. In an article in *Time* magazine about pregnancy resource centers, writer Nancy Gibbs says: "Even among pro-life activists, there is an argument about emphasis: Do you focus on fear and guilt, to make choosing an abortion harder, or on hope and support, to make 'choosing life' easier?"[2] Some centers' goal is to prevent abortion at any cost, even if that means misleading women about the risks of abortion and the development of the fetus. To these pro-lifers, the ends (preventing abortion) justify the means (manipulating women in order to sway them to choose life). Other pro-lifers run their pregnancy resource centers a different way. Their goal is also to prevent abortion in women who are considering it as one of their options. However, they focus on offering support to women so that choosing to have a baby or giving the baby up for adoption is possible.

Pro-lifers work to overturn *Roe* v. *Wade* and other laws that make abortion legal. And many pro-life organizations offer help to women who face unplanned pregnancies.

The pro-life camp is aware that the techniques some pregnancy resource centers use are criticized by others. Peggy Hartshorn, president of the organization Heartbeat International, says,

"We tell women the truth: Abortion (and casual sex) can have a profound negative impact on their physical, psychological, emotional, and spiritual health."[3] Many pregnancy resource centers focus on the idea that abortion is not an easy fix all to get things back to the way things were. "We need to counter the message that abortion won't have any consequences," says Deborah Wood, CEO of a pregnancy resource center in North Carolina, in the *Time* magazine article. "That's unrealistic. All decisions have consequences."[4] Pregnancy resource centers want women to realize that they need to look at all their options and realize that abortion can have its own consequences, and that it must not be a decision made without all the information on alternatives.

Postabortion Syndrome

There is much debate between the pro-choice and pro-life sides about the psychological effects of abortion. *Postabortion syndrome* is the term many pro-lifers use to describe psychological problems that they say result from having an abortion. It is considered by some to be a form of posttraumatic stress disorder, and its symptoms can include anxiety, depression, suicidal feelings, a feeling of numbness, difficulty sleeping, guilt, and alcohol or drug abuse.

However, the scientific community does not agree about whether postabortion syndrome exists. The American Psychological Association, the authority on mental illness in the United States, does not recognize postabortion syndrome as a psychological condition in its own right. Dr. Miriam Grossman, a psychiatrist at UCLA's student health services, writes in her book *Unprotected: A Campus Psychiatrist Reveals How Political Correctness in Her Profession Endangers Every Student*, that while a majority of women do not experience psychological problems following an abortion, it is clear to her that women can experience symptoms similar to posttraumatic stress because of feelings of trauma after an abortion.[5] (The book was originally published anonymously, but after it came out, Grossman said she was the author.) Nancy Felipe Russo, Ph.D., and psychology professor, says that although postabortion syndrome is not considered a distinct disease, it "is not to say that abortion cannot be traumatic or that it has no relationship to mental health."[6] Pro-life advocates believe the professionals in psychiatry and psychology should recognize that abortion can be traumatic for some, so that women who are struggling after abortions can receive the support they need.

Pro-life activists support legislation to curtail abortions. Many also protest against pro-choice causes, like these demonstrators opposing Planned Parenthood.

Legislative Action

Pro-life politicians have made several attempts to limit the number of abortions in the United States. They have tried to pass new laws that make it easier to choose an alternative to abortion or to make sure that women have had the chance to consider alternatives before they are allowed to have a legal abortion.

One Senate bill introduced in 2007 was the Abortion Non-Discrimination Act. This bill states that a doctor can refuse to perform abortions if his or her personal beliefs are pro-life. It also says that health insurance providers can refuse to cover the costs associated with abortion.

The Right to Life Act, H.R. 618, was introduced in January 2007. The bill proposes to amend the Fourteenth Amendment to the Constitution to give "equal protection for the right to life of each born and preborn human person."[7] The bill specifies that "human personhood" begins at the moment of fertilization. The aim of this bill goes beyond amending the Constitution and looks ahead to a time when this change could be used to try to overturn *Roe* v. *Wade*. If the Fourteenth Amendment said that an embryo or fetus has the same rights as any person, the task of making abortion illegal again would be easier. In this case, the fetus would have the same rights as a woman so that having an abortion could be considered the same as committing murder.

In 2003, President George W. Bush signed the Partial Birth Abortion Ban Act into law. This law "prohibit[s] any physician or other individual from knowingly performing a partial-birth abortion, except when necessary to save the life of a mother whose life is endangered by a physical disorder, illness, or injury."[8] The Supreme Court upheld the law in April 2007.

Individual states have also implemented their own limits on abortion, requiring waiting periods, mandatory counseling, parental consent or notification, or other restrictions, as noted in the previous chapter. Pro-lifers support these measures because they believe that they give women a chance to consider alternatives to abortion. Their hope is that during a waiting period, a woman might change her mind and decide not to have an abortion. For minors who must obtain parental consent or notify their parents that they want an abortion, pro-lifers hope this added step will eliminate abortion for young people who are simply too scared to tell their parents.

Abstinence-Only Sex Education

Many pro-life advocates have religious faith at the root of their views on abortion. Many faiths that oppose abortion also oppose sexual intercourse before marriage. The best way to avoid abortion is to avoid pregnancy, and the best way to avoid pregnancy is to not have sex. Proponents of abstinence-only education also promote abstinence as the only way to completely avoid sexually transmitted diseases.

But abstinence-only education is more than simply reducing the number of teenage pregnancies and sexually transmitted diseases. Many advocates of abstinence-only education say that it aims to provide teenagers with the skills and knowledge to make healthy relationship and sexuality decisions through-out life. Valerie Huber, executive director of the National Abstinence Education Association says, "We're not talking about just avoiding pregnancy or just avoiding teen birth. We're talking about healthy relationship building. We're talking about skills in healthy decision making, goal setting and providing information on [sexually transmitted diseases], their cause and how to prevent them."[9] The abstinence-only curriculum includes lessons that do more than tell students not to have sexual intercourse outside of marriage. They provide students with information about how to have healthy friendships and relationships, the difference between love and lust, how to make marriage work, peer pressure, and how to assert oneself, to name a few. One goal is to arm students with the information they need to build a life that is healthy and full of potential.

Disability Advocates

Pro-lifers are especially active in advocating for the disabled. What does disability have to do with abortion? With advances in medical care, doctors can now detect a wide range of fetal disabilities during pregnancy. Some women who learn the fetus is developing abnormally decide to have an abortion. They feel that abortion will prevent the suffering of a child and sometimes suffering of the would-be parents, too.

The types of fetal abnormalities doctors can detect are wide-ranging. Some disorders, such as Down syndrome and Tay-Sachs disease, result in varying degrees of physical and mental development delays and shortened life span. Other disorders can make it impossible for a baby born with that disorder to survive for even a few days. One example is Trisomy 13, a disorder that causes severe mental retardation, physical deformities, brain deformities, and other problems that can affect all the systems of the body. If a baby is born with Trisomy 13, he or she rarely survives beyond the infant stage. A woman who learns her fetus has any of these genetic abnormalities can choose to have an abortion and, if she wishes, try for another pregnancy in which she hopes the fetus will develop normally.

But pro-lifers, especially pro-lifers who are also disability advocates, believe that aborting a fetus because it has a genetic disorder or physical abnormality is wrong. They believe that it sends the message that disabled people who are living would be better off having never been born. Instead, they believe that life as a disabled person is worthwhile and fulfilling.

Fetal Pain

Pro-lifers also contend that a fetus has the ability to feel pain, and that abortion can cause suffering to the fetus. Since a fetus

Disability Rights

Pro-life activist and musician Tony Melendez is an advocate for disability rights. Melendez was a "thalidomide baby": a child born to a mother who took the drug thalidomide during pregnancy, which was later discovered to cause severe birth defects (see Chapter 2). Melendez was born in Nicaragua without arms, and he learned to play the guitar using his feet while he was in high school. He performed in church functions, and was asked to play for Pope John Paul II in 1987. He is married with two children and tours the United States and Latin America with his group, Toe Jam Music.

Tony Melendez plays the guitar in a telethon to raise money for disabled children.

cannot tell scientists whether it experiences pain, it is difficult for anyone to know for sure whether a fetus can feel pain caused by an abortion. Many medical doctors have done studies to try to determine whether the structures of the human body that are involved in sensing pain are present in a human fetus. According to London's Medical Research Council: "At present, it is not possible to pinpoint a brain area that requires maturation before a fetus or infant can feel pain."[10] A review of facts published in *The Journal of the American Medical Association* says evidence of fetal pain is limited, but it is unlikely that a fetus can feel pain before the third trimester.[11] However, some people accused the authors of the report of being biased because two of the five authors of the report, including the lead author, are active in pro-choice activities.[12] Because it is difficult to determine if a fetus feels pain, given our current knowledge of fetal development, pro-lifers are working to make sure women who do have abortions are given the option of reducing potential fetal pain after twenty weeks with medication. As Dr. R. Frank Wright writes: "We should err on the side of pain prevention."[13]

In January 2007, Senator Sam Brownback, a Republican from Kansas, introduced a bill called the Unborn Child Pain Awareness Act. The bill proposes that abortion providers who are counseling women past twenty weeks of pregnancy must make them aware that, after twenty weeks of pregnancy, "an unborn child has the physical structures necessary to experience pain."[14] The bill goes on to state that a woman must have the option of choosing to have an anesthetic or painkiller given to the fetus before the abortion.[15]

Fathers' Rights

Since women are the ones who become pregnant and ultimately decide whether to have an abortion, sometimes men get lost in the shuffle. There are men whose wives or girlfriends want an abortion, but the man wants to raise the child. In 1976, the Supreme Court heard a case involving a husband's rights when his wife wants to have an abortion. In *Planned Parenthood of Central Missouri* v. *Danforth*, the high court overturned a Missouri law that said a woman had to have written permission from her husband before she could get a legal abortion. People who advocate for father's rights say the man should have some say in whether a fetus is aborted. However, under the law, a woman does not need to get the consent of the man before she has an abortion.

Protests

Pro-life activists use protest as one tool to work for the change they wish to see in the abortion laws and practices in the United States. Protests usually involve protesters standing near abortion clinics and holding signs that display pro-life or antiabortion messages. There are several different methods of protest that different groups use. One is known as sidewalk counseling. Some pro-lifers set up outside abortion clinics and make themselves available to counsel women who may not wish to go through with an abortion. Different groups have different tactics for sidewalk counseling. Some gather near a clinic with signs that identify them as offering alternatives to abortions and wait for women considering abortion to approach them. Others try to engage women who are heading toward an abortion clinic by asking her questions or reciting a pro-life message.

Fathers' Rights

In 2002, twenty-seven-year-old John Stachokus brought a father's rights case in front of a judge in Pennsylvania. He wanted his ex-girlfriend, Tanya Meyers, to be forced to carry her pregnancy to term. The first judge to hear the case gave a temporary order to Meyers saying she could not get an abortion. A week later, a second judge, Michael Conahan, dissolved the order and dismissed the case.

Often sidewalk counselors give women pro-life literature and offer them alternatives through pregnancy resource centers. Some people who engage in sidewalk counseling are extremists and yell hateful words to women who may be going to a women's health center for an abortion or for some other health service such as a routine gynecology exam. Many pro-lifers who prefer a caring message of hope, rather than these hateful messages, disagree with these tactics.

Some pro-lifers who are Catholic meet outside of abortion clinics to pray the rosary, which is a string of beads used to count prayers. They hope their presence will show women there are people who can help them explore alternatives to abortion while they pray that women will choose life.

Another method of peaceful protest is the Life Chain. On the first Sunday of every October, churches and pro-life groups across the United States and Canada meet at a designated street with pro-life signs and a prayerful atmosphere to demonstrate their opposition to abortion in their communities. Usually their meeting place is a busy street corner in the community rather than directly outside a facility that performs abortions. The words on their signs are predetermined and approved by the organization that organizes the events. Those messages include: Abortion Kills Children; Jesus Forgives and Heals; Adoption: The Loving Option; Abortion Hurts Women; Pray to End Abortion; and Life—The First Inalienable Right.[16] Life Chain holds its participants to a code of conduct, which says participants must remain peaceful and polite, should not respond to passersby who voice disagreement with their message, should stand back from the street, and must not interfere with pedestrians.

Operation Rescue is a Christian organization that prepares protests around the United States. According to their Web site, "We will work tirelessly on behalf of the unborn until America restores personhood to the pre-born!"[17] The group protests at

Pro-life activists take many different approaches getting their message across. These young people in Montana have gathered to pray outside an abortion clinic.

Graphic Imagery

Some pro-life activists use very graphic images of fetuses after abortion as a tool to shock people into changing their minds about abortion. This tactic is debated within the pro-life community. Some pro-lifers regard using these images as a harsh truth that people need to see in order to fully understand abortion. Theresa Burke, Ph.D., writes about graphic images and articulates some of the views of pro-lifers who feel differently: "I still cringe when I am present at a pro-life demonstration that displays graphic pictures of bloody and broken babies. NO ONE likes to view these pictures—especially those pro-lifers who believe that human life is sacred."[18]

abortion clinics as well as at the homes of abortion providers. They have a history of practicing civil disobedience, protesting despite laws that require them to stay a certain distance away from abortion clinics. The group also drives what they call "truth trucks" around communities that show graphic images of aborted fetuses in hopes of convincing women not to have an abortion.

In 1991, Operation Rescue carried out one of its largest protests against three abortion clinics in Wichita, Kansas. Protesters rallied outside abortion clinics for six weeks, blocking the entrances and even crawling under the tires of an abortion provider's car to keep him from pulling into work.[19] Many protesters with Operation Rescue have been arrested in their efforts of civil disobedience.

Clinic Violence

There is a small group of antiabortion extremists who use violent protest against pro-choicers, women seeking abortion, or people who provide abortions. The vast majority of pro-lifers are sickened by this violence and believe the people acting violently are not, in fact, pro-life, because they choose to endanger or take lives. People who use violent protest as a means to voice their antiabortion ideals are often referred to by politicians, pro-choice groups, pro-life groups, and the media as zealots, extremists, or even terrorists. In 1998, Dr. Barnett Slepian, an abortion provider, was shot to death in his home in New York by a sniper motivated by antiabortion ideology. The shooter, James Charles Kopp, was caught in 2001 in France and returned to the United States for trial. He was sentenced to twenty-five years to life in prison.

The majority of pro-life activists oppose violence against clinics. The American Life League, a pro-life organization, states on its Web site that "the deliberate cold-blooded killing of a human being, from fertilization to natural death, is always wrong. This belief is the essence of what it means to be pro-life." Karen Swallow-Prior, a pro-life activist in the area of the 1998 New York shooting, responded to antiabortion terrorism by saying, "For anyone to even make the mistake that this could be in any way connected with the pro-life movement is a tragedy for the movement. Whoever did this was not acting on a pro-life principle."[20] Priests for Life, another pro-life group, offers rewards of fifty thousand dollars for information that can lead to arrests of suspects accused of shooting abortion providers.

Although pro-lifers disagree somewhat on the tactics to use to campaign against abortion, one central message is clear to all members of the pro-life community: The lives of unborn babies are sacred and must not be disposed of simply because it is more convenient for the woman. As the abortion debate changes to face advances in technology and science, pro-lifers work to craft a message that aims to change as many minds as possible and prevent abortion at every turn.

Opinions From the Middle Ground

Isabella was sixteen years old when she found out that she was pregnant. She arranged to meet her mom in a park to break the news, and before Isabella said anything, her mom said, "Please don't tell me you're pregnant." After discussing her options with her family and spending a lot of time thinking things over, Isabella chose to continue her pregnancy and place the baby for adoption. "I saw him as a gift delivered to the wrong address," Isabella says.

Isabella worked with adoption agencies to prepare for the adoption process, and to choose a family for her child. She wanted the couple adopting her child to be part Latino and part Caucasian, to be married and both have jobs, to both have college *degrees, and to be between thirty and forty years old. When she met the couple that would adopt her child, "we sparked immediately," she says. They chose an open adoption, which means the family and Isabella could stay in touch before and after the adoption. The couple was at the hospital when Isabella gave birth. "It was the most horrible experience, that anticipation of [my son] leaving," Isabella said, crying. When the adoptive parents came to take the baby away, Isabella says she "started crying, because I knew it was the end. My time with him was done."*

The weeks after Isabella had the baby were difficult. She had to be hospitalized for a complication relating to giving birth, and she was put in the maternity ward, surrounded by mothers and their new babies. She received counseling from the adoption agency and was able to return to school two weeks later. Now, Isabella's birth son is a teenager and they are involved in the big events of each other's lives.

However, Isabella's story does not end there. Four years after she gave birth the first time, Isabella got married, and she and her husband had a daughter. When their daughter was still just an infant, Isabella learned that she was pregnant again. She was surprised, because she had been using birth control. Her previous pregnancies had been very difficult emotionally, and Isabella had suffered medical complications with both. Things were not going well in Isabella's job or her husband's, and money was tight. "It was devastating for us," Isabella says, but the couple took several weeks to think about their situation. They decided to terminate the pregnancy.

During the abortion procedure, Isabella says she cried tears of "utter grief. It was a distinct wail—I don't think I'll ever forget that sound I made." The procedure cost two hundred dollars, which was half of Isabella's monthly salary. "We had to decide between the procedure and buying food," she says. Although it was not an ideal situation, Isabella and her husband both know in their souls that they made the right decision.

Now, Isabella and her husband have another child and have bought a house. Isabella finished her college degree, a goal she set for herself when she was sixteen and pregnant. She now holds a bachelor of arts degree in psychology with a minor in Chicano and Latino studies. Isabella's road was not easy, but she says, "I never regretted any choices I made."[1]

Examining Opinions

When we look at two sides to any issue, it is tempting to believe that most people's beliefs fall easily into one side or the other. But not everyone who is pro-choice believes every single idea that makes up the pro-choice position in general. The same is true for people who are pro-life—not all of them endorse every pro-life position. Between the two extremes, there is a lot of middle ground. The exact statistics about how many people in the United States support abortion vary a little depending on the study. Here are the results of two different polls taken in January 2006:

Whether you think that abortion should be legal or not, how do you feel about the morality of abortion? Is abortion always morally wrong, usually morally wrong, usually morally acceptable, or always morally acceptable?[2]	
always morally wrong	22.6%
usually morally wrong	44.2%
usually morally acceptable	27.8%
always morally acceptable	4.1%
not sure	1.3%

What is your personal feeling about abortion? It should be permitted in all cases; it should be permitted, but subject to greater restrictions than it is now; it should be permitted only in cases such as rape, incest, and to save the woman's life; it should only be permitted to save the woman's life; or it should not be permitted at all.[3]

permitted in all cases	27%
greater restrictions	15%
rape/ incest/ save woman's life	33%
only to save woman's life	17%
not permitted at all	5%
don't know/ no answer	3%

The first poll shows that only 24.7 percent of people identify with the extreme sides of the spectrum: that abortion is *always* morally wrong or *never* morally wrong. The other 75.3 percent either do not know (1.3 percent) or believe in some middle ground, where abortion is sometimes morally wrong, but sometimes morally acceptable. In the second poll, only 5 percent of people questioned believed abortion should never be allowed in any circumstance; 3 percent were not sure. That is 92 percent of people who believe that in certain cases, abortion should be allowed. A great majority of people fall somewhere in the middle of the issue of abortion.

No One Is Pro-Abortion

In the heated debate of abortion rights, no one is seriously arguing that abortion is a good thing that more women ought

The Issues at a Glance

ISSUE	PRO-CHOICE POSITION	PRO-LIFE POSITION	MIDDLE GROUND
Abortifacients	Support use of safe, legal abortifacients, such as those used in medication abortion.	Never support abortifacients; the most conservative pro-lifers also oppose agents such as birth control pills.	Most people who support abortion in some cases do not have a problem with abortifacients.
Abortion for fetal defects	Support safe, legal abortion for any reason, including for fetal defects.	Most oppose abortion for fetal defects, especially ones that are not life-threatening to the fetus.	Many support abortion for fetal defects, but fewer support it in cases where the defect is not life-threatening to the fetus.
Abortion in cases of rape and incest	Support abortion for any reason, including cases of rape or incest.	Some do not oppose abortion in cases of rape and incest.	Most people support abortion in cases of rape and incest.
Abortion to preserve health or save a woman's life	Support abortion for any reason, including preservation of a woman's health or life.	Most support abortion to save a woman's life, but the most conservative may oppose abortion to preserve a woman's health.	Many people support abortion to preserve a woman's health or save her life.
Access to birth control	Believe that birth control is necessary to prevent unwanted pregnancies.	Many support the use of methods such as condoms and spermicides; some disapprove of methods such as the IUD. Some do not support any type of artificial birth control.	Most forms of birth control are considered acceptable.
Clinic protests	Oppose clinic protests and work to ensure the safety of the clients who use clinics and the clinic staff.	Generally support and participate in clinic protests; may disagree on the appropriate tactics to use.	Most are not protesters themselves. Opinions vary widely between opposing all protest and supporting most forms of peaceful protest.
Clinic violence	Vehemently oppose violence against abortion clinics or the people involved in them.	Vast majority vehemently oppose violence against abortion clinics or the people involved in them. Very few participate in or approve of violence against clinics, staff, or patients.	Vast majority vehemently oppose violence against abortion clinics, staff, or patients.

ISSUE	PRO-CHOICE POSITION	PRO-LIFE POSITION	MIDDLE GROUND
Crisis pregnancy centers	Often criticize crisis pregnancy centers.	Many use crisis pregnancy centers to reach out to pregnant women and offer assistance that may allow them to continue their pregnancies.	Most people support financial and social assistance to pregnant women who want to continue their pregnancies; many question tactics of some centers.
Fathers' rights	Many believe that men should not be able to prevent an abortion because a woman alone must bear all the physical consequences of pregnancy and childbirth.	Many believe that men have just as much at stake in a pregnancy as women, and they should have equal right to prevent an abortion and participate in parenthood.	Some believe fathers should have a role in deciding about abortion in a perfect world but say that allowing a man to force a woman to continue a pregnancy violates her rights.
Late-term abortions	Many believe that late-term abortions are necessary in some cases and advocate for a woman's access to late-term abortion.	Oppose late-term abortion, especially D&X.	Some believe late-term abortion is allowable in the case of extreme risks to a woman, but do not advocate late-term abortions for most other reasons.
Mandatory counseling	Many believe this is an obstacle designed to prevent women from obtaining abortions.	Many believe this gives women a chance to rethink the decision to have an abortion.	Opinions about mandatory counseling vary.
Parental notification/ permission	Many regard this as an unnecessary obstacle to abortion.	Many see this as a positive step toward reducing abortions.	Opinions divided; 48% support notification/ permission; 47% oppose it.[4]
Sex education	Advocate for sex education that covers birth control, STDs, pregnancy, and abortion.	Many often advocate for abstinence-only education.	Many advocate for a mix between the two types of sex education.
Waiting periods	Many condemn waiting periods as an obstacle to women.	Many support waiting periods as a tool to decrease abortions.	Opinions vary.

to do. Pro-lifers obviously do not support abortion. And most pro-choicers also would like to see the number of abortions in the United States drastically decline. The number of abortions that were reported to the Centers for Disease Control and Prevention in 2003 was 848,163, the most recent data available as of this writing.[5] Senator Hillary Rodham Clinton said in a speech, "I believe we can all recognize that abortion in many ways represents a sad, even tragic choice to many, many women."[6]

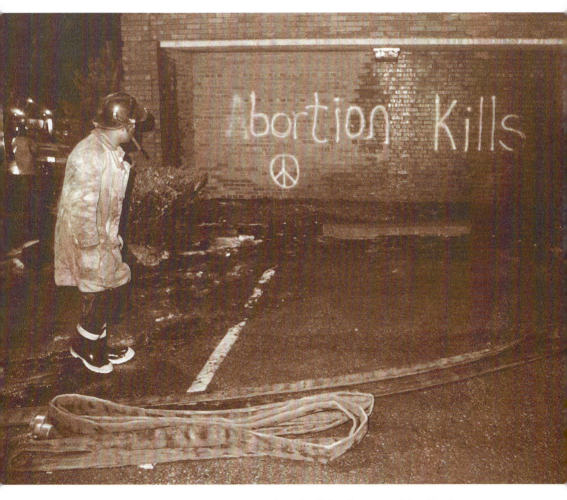

A fireman walks by a Planned Parenthood clinic destroyed by fire in Minneapolis in 1977. Most pro-lifers oppose violent tactics to fight abortion.

Finding Common Ground

Some pro-life and pro-choice groups have been able to meet with one another to talk about their differences of opinion, and to find common beliefs, in very positive ways. The Public Conversations Project was one such instance. Started by a group of family therapists in Boston, the project developed a program to teach people how to facilitate open dialogue between the two sides. The aim of the groups was to calm the sometimes volatile environment between pro-choicers and pro-lifers. When people had a chance to talk to people with opposing viewpoints, they found that they were curious and eager to understand the other perspective. Everyone was aware that the goal of the discussions was not so that one side could persuade the other. The people who participated in these talks said that the stereotypes they held about the other group were softened by the experience.[7]

A great majority of people fall somewhere in the middle on the issue of abortion: 92 percent believe that it should be allowed in certain cases.

The Common Ground Network for Life and Choice is another organization in which people from both sides come together. According to the network, "the goal of the search for common ground is to transform the dynamics of the abortion conflict, not to settle or resolve the conflict."[8]

Prevention

Both sides agree that the best way to reduce the number of abortions is for fewer women to face unplanned pregnancy. Republican Congressman Christopher Shays says, "Whatever one's views on abortion, I believe we all can recognize the importance of preventing . . . unintended pregnancies."[9]

Bipartisan legislation to try to meet this goal has been supported by both Democrats and Republicans. In 1970, George H. W. Bush and Senator Mark Hatfield, a Republican from Oregon, introduced a bill that would provide access to information and contraceptives to anyone who wanted them, with particular emphasis on low-income individuals who might not have other ways of getting them. It was signed into law by President Richard Nixon, and is known as Title X of the Public Health Service Act. The program gives money to clinics to provide patient education and counseling, breast and pelvic examinations, screenings for sexually transmitted disease and HIV, and pregnancy diagnosis and counseling.

Supporting Women and Families

When a woman faces an unplanned pregnancy, she needs to know all the information about her situation so she can make the choice that is best for her. Many Democrats, Republicans, pro-choicers, and pro-lifers want women who wish to continue their pregnancies and become mothers to have the resources needed to make that possible.

One bill introduced to make it easier for women who choose to continue pregnancy is the Pregnant Woman Support Act, introduced in September 2006 into the House of Representatives by Representative Lincoln Davis, a Democrat from Tennessee. This bill would provide a number of resources to pregnant women specifically designed to help lower the abortion rate in the United States.

The bill aims to support pregnant women and new mothers, particularly teenage parents, in many ways. It extends the State Children's Health Insurance Program (SCHIP) to allow states to include unborn children to be covered on the federally funded health-care program. It also prohibits individual health insurance plans from excluding pregnancy coverage. The way the law works now, if a woman starts a new health insurance plan while she is pregnant, the new health insurance plan can choose not to cover any pregnancy-related expenses, because they are "preexisting." This bill would not allow health

On both the pro-life and pro-choice sides of the abortion debate, many people support efforts to help women who want to continue their pregnancies.

insurance companies to discriminate against pregnant women by denying coverage or imposing higher premiums—the money a woman must pay out of pocket before her health insurance will begin to pay. The Pregnant Woman Support Act also allows for grants so new mothers under twenty years of age can receive free home nurse visits. The act also provides services to pregnant women and mothers who are victims of domestic abuse or stalking and increases food stamp eligibility.

This piece of legislation also places emphasis on continuing educational opportunities for pregnant teens and young mothers. It requires new programs to help pregnant and parenting teens to finish their high-school education. In addition, it allows grants for pregnant women and mothers to receive financial assistance to go to college. In order to also support women choosing adoption, the act expands adoption tax credit and adoption assistance programs.

Postabortion Syndrome

In an article in *The New York Times Magazine*, social worker Ava Torre-Bueno presents a moderate perspective on postabortion syndrome. She says: "What you hear in the [pro-choice] movement is 'Let's not make noise about this' and 'Most women are fine, I'm sure you will be too.' And that is unfair."[10] Although some people do not recognize postabortion syndrome as its own psychological condition, most people empathize with a woman who is having trouble after an abortion and advocate that mental health care be accessible to women—and indeed anyone suffering from depression, anxiety, or other symptoms.

In an ideal world, abortion would be unnecessary because every pregnancy would be planned, every pregnant woman would be healthy, and every fetus would be developing normally. Unfortunately, that is not the world in which we live. As long as abortion is in demand, there will be controversy surrounding it. But when the two sides of the issue can come together and work toward common goals like supporting women and preventing unplanned pregnancy, many hope the hostility of the abortion debate can take a backseat.

6 **Abortion in the Twenty-first Century**

The dialogue about the abortion issue in the United States will continue to evolve as new technologies emerge for fetal testing, as well as new uses for fetal tissues are discovered. The politics of abortion will continue to change as new politicians are elected.

Advances in Medical Technology

Although abortion has been an issue for centuries, it would seem as though the issues should be well established, but technology continues to change the face of the abortion debate. New medicines, medical research, and advances in the treatment of infertility make abortion a relevant topic in the twenty-first century.

Modern medicine has changed the way women choose whether to continue their pregnancies. Doctors can now determine whether a fetus will be born with specific genetic illnesses or disabilities. There are a few ways doctors can make these diagnoses. One is with a test called amniocentesis. In this test, medical staff extract a small amount of amniotic fluid—the fluid that surrounds and cushions a fetus in the womb—with a needle. The fluid contains cells from the fetus that can be tested for chromosomal and genetic defects, such as Down syndrome, spina bifida (a disorder of the spine), and anencephaly (incomplete or missing brain). Some genetic disorders can only be detected late in pregnancy, which makes it especially difficult for women who learn the fetus has a serious defect. Some women in this situation choose to have an abortion.

> It would seem as though the issues regarding abortion should be well established, but technology continues to change the face of the abortion debate.

Another new way that doctors test for genetic disorders is through preimplantation genetic diagnosis. This is a series of tests performed on fertilized eggs made during the in vitro fertilization process, when the ovum and sperm are joined in a petri dish. Once an egg is fertilized by the sperm, the cells are allowed to divide for about three days, when it becomes an eight- to ten-cell mass called a blastocyst. To test for genetic abnormalities, technicians carefully extract one cell from the blastocyst. Medical staff can learn a lot from that one cell. They can see whether the blastocyst has malformations that would lead to a wide variety of genetic diseases. If they find a blastocyst that shows signs of a genetic disease, the doctors discard that blastocyst so that it is not implanted into the woman to try to establish a pregnancy. That way, doctors can implant only the healthiest blastocysts during in vitro fertilization. Preimplantation genetic diagnosis is controversial. Several countries have laws banning or limiting preimplantation genetic diagnosis, including Italy, England, Germany, and France. The process can determine the gender of fertilized eggs, so some people might try to use it because they prefer to have either a boy or a girl. Some people who advocate for the disabled oppose preimplantation diagnosis. They say that destroying fertilized eggs because the baby that could be born would be disabled implies that people with disabilities should never have been born.

Stem-cell research is another area that is affected by the same issues as the abortion debate. Stem cells are the cells that make up blastocysts (fertilized eggs). During the in vitro fertilization, many blastocysts are made in the hopes that just one or two will survive and turn into viable pregnancies. Often there are left over blastocysts. A couple may have twenty fertilized eggs and achieve successful pregnancies and births after using just some of the fertilized eggs. These "leftovers" are usually disposed of as medical waste. But scientists can use these extra fertilized eggs to perform research that they hope will lead to the cures of many diseases and defects, such as paralysis after spinal injuries, multiple sclerosis, Parkinson's disease, and others. Pro-lifers generally oppose stem-cell research because they say it is not justifiable to use one life to research cures that could save others.

The Future of Abortion in Politics

The status of abortion law will always be questioned as Democratic and Republican majorities in Congress are in a state of flux, as well as the appointment of Supreme Court justices. This means that the balance of Democrats and Republicans in Congress can make a big difference in how abortion laws are shaped in the United States. If a majority of the members of the U.S. Senate and House of Representatives is Democratic, laws that support a woman's right to choose

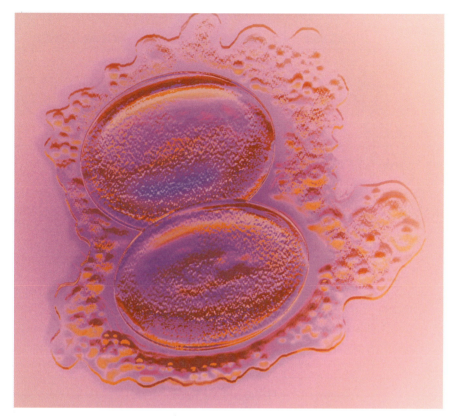

A two-celled embryo, shortly after fertilization. Pro-lifers are generally opposed to embryonic stem cell research because embryos are destroyed in the process.

abortion are more likely to prevail. Conversely, if a majority of members of Congress are Republican, the laws putting limits on abortion are more likely to be passed.

The president's feelings on abortion are also extremely important. One reason is that if a bill that deals with abortion passes Congress, the president can veto it; it takes a two-thirds majority of Congress to override a veto. But even more important than veto power is the president's duty to appoint justices to the U.S. Supreme Court. The Supreme Court is the highest court in the United States and has a great deal of power in shaping the most controversial issues that the United States

Supreme Court justice	Birth date	Appointed by	View on Abortion
John Roberts (chief justice)	January 27, 1955	George W. Bush	Has never defined his stance clearly, but most people believe he would not overturn *Roe* v. *Wade.*
John Paul Stevens	April 20, 1920	Gerald Ford	Supports abortion rights.
Antonin Scalia	March 11, 1936	Ronald Reagan	Believes abortion laws should be decided by each state; also believes *Roe* v. *Wade* was wrongly decided and should be overturned.
Anthony Kennedy	July 23, 1936	Ronald Reagan	Has upheld a woman's right to have an abortion, but has voted to put more restrictions on abortion.
David Souter	September 17, 1939	George H.W. Bush	Has upheld a woman's right to have an abortion, but has voted to put more restrictions on abortion.
Clarence Thomas	June 23, 1948	George H.W. Bush	Opposes abortion and has voted to restrict it as much as possible. Believes *Roe* v. *Wade* was wrongly decided and should be overturned.
Ruth Bader Ginsberg	March 15, 1933	Bill Clinton	Supports abortion rights.
Stephen Breyer	August 15, 1938	Bill Clinton	Has consistently upheld abortion rights.
Samuel Alito	April 1, 1950	George W. Bush	Is personally opposed to abortion, but has said he would approach cases about abortion with an open mind.

faces, including abortion. Supreme Court justices have lifelong appointments, meaning that they will be on the Court either until they choose to retire or until they die. Supreme Court justices can be impeached if they do something wrong, but that has only happened one time in U.S. history. When a Supreme Court justice leaves the bench, the president appoints a new Supreme Court justice, and members of the Senate confirm or reject the person nominated.

The Supreme Court has played a vital role in how abortion laws are made. A president's feelings about abortion are important because if a new vacancy in the Supreme Court comes up during the president's term, the president may consider potential candidates' views on abortion as he or she decides whom to appoint. In this way, the president has tremendous power over the abortion laws in the country. With four Supreme Court justices over the age of seventy, the next two presidential terms are likely to bring new Supreme Court nominees.

Will *Roe* v. *Wade* Be Overturned?

Many people wonder whether the Supreme Court decision that made abortion legal might be overturned by the Supreme Court one day. Many people believe that rather than trying to overturn *Roe* v. *Wade*, pro-life lawmakers will instead try to "chip away" at it, adding new restrictions to the laws that will make abortion technically legal, but so difficult to obtain that it is not actually a real option for many women.

Abortion is an uncomfortable topic, and many people simply avoid talking about it so they will not be forced to deal with the issue head-on. However, it is important to be able to discuss the issues that shape our laws and our country. Abortion is not going anywhere, regardless of whether laws prohibit it. Only by discussing abortion can the citizens of the United States continue to seek common ground.

Chapter Notes

Chapter 1 Abortion: Opposing Viewpoints

1. Personal interview, March 20, 2007.
2. L. B. Finer and S. K. Henshaw, "Disparities in rates of unintended pregnancy in the United States, 1994 and 2001," *Perspectives on Sexual and Reproductive Health*, 2006, 38(2): 90–96.
3. Lilo T. Strauss et al., "Abortion Surveillance—United States, 2003," Centers for Disease Control and Prevention Division of Reproductive Health, National Center for Chronic Disease Prevention and Health Promotion, November 24, 2006, <http://www.cdc.gov/mmwr/preview/mmwrhtml/ss5511a1.htm> (March 23, 2007).
4. Ibid.
5. U.S. Library of Medicine/National Institutes of Health, "Fetal Development," *Medline Plus Medical Encyclopedia*, n.d., <http://www.nlm.nih.gov/medlineplus/ency/article/002398.htm> (January 13, 2007).
6. U.S. Library of Medicine/National Institutes of Health, "First Trimester Pregnancy," *Medline Plus Medical Encyclopedia*, n.d., <http://www.nlm.nih.gov/medlineplus/ency/article/000887.htm> (February 28, 2007).
7. U.S. Library of Medicine/National Institutes of Health, "Fetal Development," *Medline Plus Medical Encyclopedia*, n.d., <http://www.nlm.nih.gov/medlineplus/ency/article/002398.htm> (January 13, 2007).
8. Ibid.
9. "Baby as Small as Pen When Born to Go Home," Reuters, February 20, 2007, <http://www.nytimes.com/reuters/news/news-usababy.html?_r=2&oref=slogin&oref=slogin> (February 28, 2007).
10. "Miscarriage," *March of Dimes Quick Reference and Fact Sheet*, n.d., <http://www.marchofdimes.com/professionals/14332_1192.asp> (February 17, 2007).
11. "First Trimester Options," Planned Parenthood, n.d., <http://www.plannedparenthood.org/birth-control-pregnancy/abortion/first-trimester options.htm> (February 18, 2007).
12. "Summary Report: Early Reproductive Events and Breast Cancer Workshop," National Cancer Institute: U.S. National Institutes of Health, n.d., <http://www.cancer.gov/cancerinfo/ere-workshop-report> (February 18, 2007).

13. "U.S. FDA grants OTC status to Barr's Plan B emergency contraceptive," *FDA Law Weekly*, September 21, 2006, p. 5.

14. "When Does Life Begin?" The Harris Poll, *HarrisInteractive*, n.d., <http://www.harrisinteractive.com/NEWS/allnewsbydate.asp?NewsID=94> (February 18, 2007).

15. Ibid.

Chapter 2   Abortion Throughout History

1. Glenc F. Entrez Pub Med., Abstract to "Induced abortion—a historical outline," Polski Tygodnik Lekarski, November 11, 1974, pp. 1957–1958, <http://www.ncbi.nlm.nih.gov/entrez/query.fcgi?cmd=Retrieve&db=PubMed&list_uids=4610534&dopt=Abstract> (February 19, 2007).

2. Malcolm Potts and Martha Campbell, "History of Contraception," *Gynecology and Obstetrics*, vol. 6, chap. 8, 2002, <http://big.berkeley.edu/ifplp.history.pdf> (March 13, 2007).

3. Soranus, *Gynaecology*, n.d., <http://www.stoa.org/diotima/anthology/wlgr/wlgr-medicine355.shtml> (March 13, 2007).

4. Claudia Dreifus, "The Dalai Lama," *The New York Times*, November 28, 1993, p. 52.

5. Sandhya Jain, "The Right to Family Planning, Contraception and Abortion: The Hindu View," in *Sacred Rights: The Case for Contraception and Abortion in World Religions*, Daniel C. Maguire, ed. (New York: Oxford University Press, 2003), pp. 135–136.

6. Sa'diyya Khilafah, "Family Planning, Contraception, and Abortion in Islam," in *Sacred Rights: The Case for Contraception and Abortion in World Religions*, Daniel C. Maguire, ed. (New York: Oxford University Press, 2003), pp. 120–123.

7. Laurie Zoloth, "Each One an Entire World: A Jewish Perspective on Family Planning," in *Sacred Rights: The Case for Contraception and Abortion in World Religions*, Daniel C. Maguire, ed. (New York: Oxford University Press, 2003), pp. 40–43.

8. Jerry L. Van Marter and Evan Silverstein, "General Assembly Backgrounder: Abortion," Presbyterian News Service Office of Communications, n.d., <http://www.pcusa.org/pcnews/2006/06291.htm> (March 16, 2007).

9. SBC Position Statement, "Sanctity of Life," n.d., <http://www.sbc.net/aboutus/pssanctity.asp> (March 16, 2007).

10. John L. Allen, Jr., "Under Vatican ruling, abortion triggers automatic excommunication," *National Catholic Reporter*, January 17, 2003,

<http://ncronline.org/NCR_Online/archives/011703/011703d.htm> (March 16, 2007).

11. Leslie J. Reagan, *When Abortion Was a Crime: Women, Medicine and Law in the United States, 1867–1973* (Berkeley, Calif.: University of California Press, 1997), p. 26.

12. Ibid., p. 78.

13. Rickie Solinger, *Pregnancy Power: A Short History of Reproductive Politics in America* (New York: New York University Press, 2005), p. 71.

14. N. E. H. Hull, William James Hoffer, and Peter Charles Hoffer, *The Abortion Rights Controversy in America: A Legal Reader* (Chapel Hill, N.C.: The University of North Carolina Press, 2004), p. 29.

15. U.S. National Library of Medicine and National Institutes of Health, "Congenital Rubella." *Medline Plus Medical Encyclopedia*, n.d., <http://www.nlm.nih.gov/medlineplus/ency/article/001658.htm> (March 23, 2007).

16. Carl N. Flanders, *Library in a Book: Abortion.* (New York: Facts On File, 1991), p. 7.

17. Reagan, p. 237.

18. "History of Abortion," National Abortion Federation, n.d., <http://www.prochoice.org/about_abortion/history_abortion.html> (April 2, 2007).

19. Christine Vestal, "States probe limits of abortion policy," *Stateline.org.*, n.d., <http://www.stateline.org/live/ViewPage.action?siteNodeId=136&languageId=1&contentId=121780> (April 2, 2007).

20. Ibid.

21. N. E. H. Hull and Peter Charles Hoffer, *Roe* v. *Wade: The Abortion Rights Controversy in American History* (Lawrence, Kans.: University of Kansas Press, 2001), p. 190.

22. U.S. Supreme Court, "*Doe* v. *Bolton*, 410 U.S. 179 (1973)," *FindLaw*, n.d., <http://caselaw.lp.findlaw.com/scripts/getcase.pl?court=us&vol=410&invol=179> (April 3, 2007).

23. Hull, Hoffer, and Hoffer, p. 229.

24. Vestal.

25. Hull, Hoffer, and Hoffer, p. 250.

26. Supreme Court. "*Stenberg* v. *Carhart* (99-830) 530 U.S. 914 (2000)." *Cornell Law School: Legal Information Institute*, n.d., <http://www.law.cornell.edu/supct/html/99-830.ZS.html> (April 3, 2007).

27. Vestal.

28. Hull and Hoffer, p. 191.

29. Flanders, p. 104.

30. Ibid., p. 100.

31. Hull and Hoffer, p. 260.

32. Bill Clinton, *Between Hope and History* (New York: Random House, 1996), p. 137.

33. "President Signs Partial Birth Abortion Ban Act of 2003," November 2003, <http://www.whitehouse.gov/news/releases/2003/11/20031105-1.html> (April 3, 2007).

34. "Safe Abortion: Technical and Policy Guidance for Health Systems," World Health Organization, 2003, p. 7, <http://www.who.int/reproductive-health/publications/safe_abortion/safe_abortion.pdf> (April 3, 2007).

35. Ibid.

36. United States Supreme Court opinion, p. 2, drafted by Justice Kennedy, <http://www.supremecourtus.gov/opinions/06pdf/05-380.pdf> (April 18, 2007).

37. United States Supreme Court dissent, p. 3, drafted by Justice Ginsberg, <http://www.supremecourtus.gov/opinions/06pdf/05-380.pdf p. 51> (April 18, 2007).

38. "NAF Violence and Disruption Statistics," National Abortion Federation, March 2007, <http://www.prochoice.org/pubs_research/publications/downloads/about_abortion/violence_statistics.pdf> (April 3, 2007).

39. Personal interview, April 1, 2007.

Chapter 3 The Pro-Choice Argument

1. Personal interview, April 3, 2007.

2. "Abortion Facts: Access to Abortion," National Abortion Federation, n.d., <http://www.prochoice.org/about_abortion/facts/access_abortion.html> (March 17, 2007).

3. Planned Parenthood Federation of America, *Annual Report 2005–2006*, <http://www.plannedparenthood.org/files/PPFA/Annual_report.pdf> (October 31, 2007).

4. Personal interview, April 2007.

5. "About the Issues: Lack of Training," Medical Students for Choice, n.d., <http://www.ms4c.org/issuetraining.htm> (March 16, 2007).

6. Personal interview, April 1, 2007.

7. "Parental Consent/Notification Requirements for Minors Seeking Abortions, as of June 2006," The Henry Kaiser Family Foundation, n.d., <http://www.statehealthfacts.org/comparetable.jsp?ind=460&cat=10> (March 16, 2007).

8. Ibid.

9. "Mandatory Waiting Period and Information Requirements for Women Seeking Abortions, as of December 9, 2005," The Henry Kaiser Family Foundation, n.d., <http://www.statehealthfacts.org/comparetable.jsp?ind=459&cat=10> (March 3, 2007).

10. Ibid.

11. Access to Legal Pharmaceuticals Act. H. R. 1652, n.d., <http://thomas.loc.gov/cgi-bin/query/z?c109:H.R.1652:> (March 27, 2007).

12. "The Oral Contraceptive Controversy," American Association of Pro-Life Obstetricians and Gynecologists, June 15, 2000,<http://www.aaplog.org/oral.htm> (March 27, 2007).

13. "Laws Affecting Reproductive Health and Rights: Trends in the States 2006," Alan Guttmacher Institute, © 1996–2006, <http://www.guttmacher.org/statecenter/updates/2006/overview.html> (October 20, 2007).

14. Social Security Administration, Social Security Act: Title V: Maternal and Child Health Services Black Grant, Separate Program for Abstinence Education, Section 510 [42 U.S.C. 710], n.d., <http://www.ssa.gov/OP_Home/ssact/title05/0510.htm> (April 17, 2007).

15. Office of Management and Budget, "Budget of the United States Government, FY 2008," Washington: Government Printing Office, n.d., <http://www.whitehouse.gov/omb/budget/fy2008/hhs.html> (March 27, 2007).

16. Personal interview, April 3, 2007.

17. Christopher Trenholm et al., *Impacts of Four Title V, Section 510 Abstinence Education Programs: Final Report,* Mathematica Policy Research, Inc., April 2007, pp. xvii and xx.

18. "In brief: Facts on Induced Abortion in the United States," Alan Guttmacher Institute, May 2006, <http://www.guttmacher.org/pubs/fb_induced_abortion.html#3> (March 26, 2007).

19. *Brandi Standridge* v. *Union Pacific*, 06-1706 8th Circuit March 15, 2007, <http://www.ca8.uscourts.gov/opndir/07/03/061706P.pdf> (March 19, 2007).

20. "Federally Funded Pregnancy Resource Centers Mislead Teens about Abortion Risks," Committee on Oversight and Government Reform, Henry R. Waxman, Chairman, July 17, 2006, <http://oversight.house.gov/story.asp?ID=1080> (October 31, 2007).

21. Amy Bryant, "Stopping Crisis Pregnancy Centers," April 20, 2006, Planned Parenthood, n.d., <http://www.plannedparenthood.org/news-articles-press/politics-policy-issues/abortion-access/pregnancy-centers-6174.htm> (March 28, 2007).

22. United States House of Representatives Committee on Government Reform—Minority Staff, Special Investigations Committee, "False and Misleading Health Information Provided by Federally Funded Pregnancy Resource Centers," July 2006, <http://oversight.house.gov/Documents/20060717101140-30092.pdf> (March 24, 2007).

23. Personal interview, April 9, 2007.

24. Alexander Sanger, *Beyond Choice: Reproductive Freedom in the 21st Century* (New York: PublicAffairs, 2004), p. 17.

Chapter 4 The Pro-Life Argument

1. Personal interview, March 21, 2007.

2. Nancy Gibbs, "The Grassroots Abortion War," *Time*, February 15, 2007, <http://www.time.com/time/magazine/article/0,9171,1590444-1,00.html> (March 3, 2007).

3. Peggy Hartshorn, Ph.D., "Truths Taught by Heartbeat Acknowledged by UCLA Psychiatrist," *LifeLines: An Update for Lifesaver*, February 2007, <http://www.heartbeatinternational.org/eNewsletter/enews_01-07-full.htm> (March 23, 2007).

4. Gibbs.

5. Anonymous, M.D., *Unprotected: A Campus Psychiatrist Reveals How Political Correctness in Her Profession Endangers Every Student* (New York: Penguin, 2006), pp. 83–89.

6. N. Crawford, "Web site puts out information on reproductive health," American Psychological Association: *Monitor on Psychology*, February 2003, <http://www.apa.org/monitor/feb03/website.html> (February 26, 2007).

7. Right to Life Act. H.R. 618, <http://thomas.loc.gov/cgibin/query/z?c110:H.R.618:> (March 26, 2007).

8. "Public Law 108–105—November 5, 2003," Washington, D.C.: Government Printing Office. n.d., <http://frwebgate.access.gpo.gov/

cgibin/getdoc.cgi?dbname=108_cong_public_laws&docid=f:publ105. 108.pdf> (February 18, 2007).

9. Kevin Freking, "Abstinence Groups Try to Maintain Funds," *USA Today*, April 10, 2007, <http://www.usatoday.com/news/washington/2007-04-10-122887527_x.htm> (April 10, 2007).

10. Medical Research Council, "Report of the MRC Expert Group on Fetal Pain," August 28, 2001, <http://www.mrc.ac.uk/Utilities/Document record/index.htm?d=MRC002413> (February 21, 2007).

11. Susan Lee, et al., "Fetal Pain: A Systematic Multidisciplinary Review of the Evidence," *The Journal of the American Medical Association*, vol. 294, no. 8, August 2005, <http://jama.ama-assn.org/cgi/content/short/294/8/947> (March 5, 2007).

12. Emily Bazar, "2 authors of fetal-pain paper accused of bias," *USAToday*, August 24, 2005, <http://www.usatoday.com/news/health/2005-08-24-fetal-pain-bias_x.htm> (February 10, 2007).

13. Frank R. White, "Are we overlooking fetal pain and suffering during abortion?" *American Society of Anesthesiologists Newsletter*, October 2001, <http://www.asahq.org/Newsletters/2001/10_01/white.htm> (February 3, 2007).

14. S.356, Unborn Child Pain Awareness Act of 2007 (Introduced in Senate), <http://thomas.loc.gov/cgi-bin/query/F?c110:1:./temp/~c110YA4LgP:e 7779:> (March 28, 2007).

15. Ibid.

16. "What Is Life Chain?" National Life Chain, n.d., <http://www.national lifechain.org/> (February 13, 2007).

17. "Will You Help?" Operation Rescue, January 1, 2004, <http://www. operationrescue.org/?p=54> (March 19, 2007).

18. Theresa Burke and J. Kevin Burke, "Let's Talk About Graphic Pictures," Priests for Life, n.d., <http://www.priestsforlife.org/ images/post-abortion-healing.htm> (March 28, 2007).

19. Isabel Wilkerson, "Drive Against Abortion Finds a Symbol: Wichita," *The New York Times*, August 4, 1991, p. 20.

20. "Acts of Hatred," A News hour with Jim Lehrer Transcript, December 31, 1998, <http://www.pbs.org/newshour/bb/health/july-dec98/abortion_12-31.html> (January 29, 2007).

Chapter 5   Opinions From the Middle Ground

1. Personal interview, April 3, 2007.

2. Hamilton College—The Arthur Levitt Public Affairs Center, January 5, 2006, Polling The Nations (March 6, 2007).

3. CBS News poll, January 9, 2006, Method: telephone. Sample Size: 1,151, accessed through Polling The Nations (March 6, 2007).

4. NBC News/ *Wall Street Journal* Poll, Washington, D.C.: National Broadcasting Company, April 6, 2005, accessed through Polling the Nations, April 4, 2007.

5. Lilo T. Strauss, et al., "Abortion Surveillance—United States, 2003," Centers for Disease Control and Prevention Division of Reproductive Health, National Center for Chronic Disease Prevention and Health Promotion, November 24, 2006, <http://www.cdc.gov/mmwr/preview/mmwrhtml/ss5511a1.htm> (March 23, 2007).

6. Remarks by Senator Hillary Rodham Clinton to the NYS Family Planning Providers, January 24, 2005, <http://clinton.senate.gov/~clinton/speeches/2005125A05.html> (February 17, 2007).

7. "An Overview of PCP's Work on Abortion," Public Conversations Project, November 30, 1999, <http://www.publicconversations.org/pcp/resource_details.php?ref_id=97> (March 12, 2007).

8. Mary Jacksteit and Dr. Adrian Kaufmann, *The Common Ground Network for Life and Choice Manual*, n.d., <http://www.sfcg.org/programmes/us/pdf/manual.pdf> (March 16, 2007).

9. "Shays Statement on 'Putting Prevention First' Act," April 21, 2004, Press release, <http://www.house.gov/shays/news/2004/april/aprppf.htm> (March 27, 2007).

10. Emily Bazelon, "Is There a Post-Abortion Syndrome? Inside the next fight over Roe v. Wade," *The New York Times Magazine*, January 21, 2007.

Glossary

abortifacient—Any substance or tool that causes an abortion, including medication or devices.

blastocyst—A stage at which a fertilized ovum, which has not been implanted, reaches between seventy and one hundred cells.

cervix—The narrow lower portion of the uterus where it meets the vaginal canal.

chromosomes—Threadlike structures that carry genetic information through an ovum or sperm cell.

ectopic pregnancy—A pregnancy in which the embryo implants outside the uterus, usually in a fallopian tube.

embryo—The stage that begins when a fertilized ovum attaches to the uterine wall, lasting until the eighth week of pregnancy.

ensoulment—The point at which a fetus becomes fully human according to some philosophies and religions.

fetus—The scientific and medical name for an implanted embryo from week eight of pregnancy until delivery.

laminaria—A type of dried seaweed that expands within the cervix to artificially dilate the cervix to prepare for an abortion procedure.

late-term abortion—Any abortion procedure performed in the later stages of pregnancy.

medication abortion—An abortion induced by means of medication rather than surgically.

methotrexate—A drug used in medication abortion that stops a pregnancy from developing further.

mifepristone—A drug used in medication abortion to thin the lining of the uterus and soften the cervix.

miscarriage—The loss of pregnancy due to natural causes.

misoprostol—A drug used in medication abortion that causes strong contractions in the uterus, forcing the embryo and tissue out of the uterus.

postabortion syndrome—A term used mainly by pro-lifers to describe psychological symptoms that occur as a result of trauma after an abortion.

quickening—The point at which a pregnant woman can feel the fetus moving inside her.

spontaneous abortion—*See* miscarriage.

surgical abortion—A procedure given after six or seven weeks of pregnancy in which the cervix is dilated and the contents of the uterus are removed. Surgical tools used may include a curette, a vacuum aspiration cannula, or other tools.

therapeutic abortion—An abortion performed to preserve the health or life of the pregnant woman.

trigger law—A state law that expresses intent to outlaw abortion if federal laws that allow abortion are overturned.

trimester—The three stages into which pregnancy is divided. The first trimester goes from implantation until week twelve; the second trimester goes from week thirteen through week twenty-four; the third trimester lasts from week twenty-five until delivery.

viability—The point in pregnancy at which a fetus is able to survive outside the womb.

zygote—The name for a fertilized ovum that begins at the moment of fertilization and lasts until the zygote reaches between seventy and one hundred cells.

For More Information

Pro-Choice Organizations

Catholics for a Free Choice
1436 U Street NW, Suite 301
Washington, DC 20009-3997
(202) 986-6093
(202) 332-7995 (fax)

Center for Reproductive Rights
120 Wall Street
New York, NY 10005
(917) 637-3600
(917) 637-3666 (fax)

NARAL Pro-Choice America
1156 15th Street, NW Suite 700
Washington, DC 20005
(202) 530-4164
(202) 973-3096 (fax)

National Abortion Federation
1660 L Street, NW, Suite 450
Washington, DC 20036
(202) 667-5881
(202) 667-5890 (fax)

Planned Parenthood Federation of America
434 West 33rd Street
New York, NY 10001
(212) 541-7800
(212) 245-1845 (fax)

Pro-Life Organizations

Democrats for Life
601 Pennsylvania Avenue, NW
South Building, Suite 900
Washington, DC 20004
(202) 220-3066
(202) 638-6957 (fax)

Feminists for Life of America
PO Box 320667
Alexandria, VA 22320
(703) 836-3354

Heartbeat International
665 East Dublin-Granville Road,
Suite 440
Columbus, OH 43229-3245
(614) 885-7577
(614) 885-8746 (fax)

National Pro-Life Alliance
4521 Windsor Arms Court
Annandale, VA 22003

National Right to Life Committee
512 10th St. NW
Washington, DC 20004
(202) 626-8800

Further Reading

Gold, Susan Dudley. *Roe* v. *Wade: A Woman's Choice.* Tarrytown, N.Y.: Benchmark Books, 2005.

Herring, Mark Y. *The Pro-Life/Choice Debate.* Westport, Conn: Greenwood Press, 2003.

Nolan, Mary. *Teen Pregnancy.* Chicago: Heinemann Library, 2003.

Powers, Meghan, ed. *The Abortion Rights Movement.* Detroit: Greenhaven Press, 2006.

Watkins, Christine, ed. *The Ethics of Abortion.* Detroit: Greenhaven Press, 2005.

Williams, Mary E., ed. *Examining the Issues Through Political Cartoons: Abortion.* San Diego, Calif.: Greenhaven Press, 2003.

Internet Addresses

Mom, Dad, I'm Pregnant

<http://www.momdadimpregnant.com/>

This Web site offers advice to teens and parents about how to have open, healthy discussions when a teen girl is pregnant (or a teen male's girlfriend is pregnant).

The Common Ground Network for Life and Choice

<http://www.sfcg.org/Programmes/us/us_life.html>

This Web site offers information about the project, as well as links to training manuals designed to help people facilitate discussion and debate on the topic of abortion.

The OYEZ Project

<http://www.oyez.org/cases/>

This Web site, sponsored by Northwestern University, offers free online audio and transcripts Supreme Court arguments, including Roe *v.* Wade, Planned Parenthood *v.* Casey, *and other abortion-related cases.*

Index

A

abortifacient, 17, 21, 83
abortion
    access, 37, 38, 42, 45, 46–47,
        50, 51, 61, 83, 84
    cost, 46, 50–51, 69, 80
    illegal, 18, 27–31, 32, 40, 41,
        45, 61, 69
    methods, 10–14, 20, 21, 27, 28,
        40, 45
    psychological effects, 35, 55, 66,
        67–68, 89
    restrictions, 34, 40, 61, 69, 82,
        93, 94, 95
Abortion Non–Discrimination Act,
    69
Access to Legal Pharmaceuticals
    Act, 53
adoption, 18, 34, 40, 63, 64, 66,
    75, 79–80, 89
Alito, Samuel, 94
amniocentesis, 91
amniotic sac, 14

B

birth control, 20, 23, 24, 28, 29,
    32, 46, 51, 53–54, 55, 56, 57,
    58, 61, 80, 83, 84
blastocyst, 8, 91–92
Bolton, Arthur K., 35
Breyer, Stephen, 40, 94
Brownback, Sam, 73
Burke, Theresa, 77
Bush, George H.W., 39, 86, 94
Bush, George W., 40, 69, 94

C

cancer, 12, 26, 46, 59

Carter, Jimmy, 38
cervix, 8, 10, 12, 13, 14
childbirth, 14, 18, 45, 54, 84
Clinton, Bill, 40, 94
Clinton, Hillary Rodham, 85
Coffee, Linda, 32
Common Ground Network for
    Life and Choice, 86
Comstock Act, 28–29
Comstock, Anthony, 28–29
Conahan, Michael, 74
conception, 22, 24, 35, 63
counseling, mandatory, 40, 48–50,
    58, 64, 69, 73, 84
crisis pregnancy center, 46, 58–59,
    64, 66–67, 84

D

Dalai Lama, 21
Davis, Lincoln, 87
Democrats, 38, 59, 86, 87, 92
Democrats for Life, 38
Denmark, 41
dilation and curettage (D&C), 13,
    14, 47
dilation and evacuation (D&E),
    13, 14
dilation and extraction (D&X), 14,
    18, 40–41, 69, 84
Doe, Mary, 35
Doe v. *Bolton*, 35

E

ectopic pregnancy, 10, 24–25
embryo, 7, 8, 9, 10, 17, 18, 19,
    24, 26, 69
emergency contraceptive pills, 15,
    17, 46, 51, 53

F

fallopian tube, 8, 10, 24, 26, 51
fathers' rights, 73–74, 84
fertilization, 8, 15, 17, 19, 21, 22, 78, 91–92
fetus, 18, 19, 24, 26, 27, 34, 36, 58, 66, 74, 77, 89
  and abortion procedures, 10–14, 40–41, 73
  defects, 21, 22, 23, 30, 31, 71, 83, 91
  development of, 7, 8–10, 14, 15
  fetal pain, 71, 73
  rights of, 45, 64, 69
  testing, 91
Finkbine, Sherri, 31
Ford, Gerald, 94
Freedom of Access to Clinic Entrances Act, 42

G

genetic disorders, 7, 71, 91–92
Ginsberg, Ruth Bader, 40, 94
Gonzales v. Carhart, 41–42
Griswold v. Connecticut, 32, 34
Grossman, Miriam, 67–68

H

Hames, Margie Pitt, 35
Hartshorn, Peggy, 66–67
Hatfield, Mark, 86–87
health insurance, 51, 53–54, 57–58, 69, 87–88
Heartbeat International, 66–67
Huber, Valerie, 70
Hyde Amendment, 51
Hyde, Henry, 34

I

incest, 7, 23, 30, 39, 40, 41, 48, 51, 82, 83
infertility, 91

in vitro fertilization, 91–92

K

Kennedy, Anthony, 94
Kopp, James Charles, 78

L

laminaria, 13, 14
late-term abortion, 14, 23, 36, 41, 84

M

Maloney, Carolyn, 59
McCorvey, Norma, 32, 34
medical advances, 7, 21, 71, 78, 90–92
Medical Students for Choice, 47
medication abortion, 10–12, 83
Melendez, Tony, 72
methotrexate, 10
Meyers, Tanya, 74
mifepristone, 10
miscarriage, 9–10, 12, 13, 17, 28
misoprostol, 10–11, 61
Model Penal Code, 30

N

NARAL Pro-Choice America, 46, 57
National Abortion Federation, 42, 46
National Abstinence Education Association, 70
Nixon, Richard, 87

O

ovulation, 15, 54

P

parental notification/consent, 40, 47–48, 50, 69–70, 84
parenting, 54, 88

partial-birth abortion. *See* dilation and extraction (D&E).
Partial Birth Abortion Ban Act of 2003, 40–41, 69
Planned Parenthood Federation of America, 35, 37, 46, 57, 59, 74
Planned Parenthood of Central Missouri v. *Danforth*, 74
Planned Parenthood v. *Casey*, 35–36, 37
Pliny the Elder, 21
Pope Gregory XIV, 24
Pope Innocent III, 24
Pope Pius IX, 24
Pope Sixtus V, 24
postabortion syndrome, 66, 67–68, 89
posttraumatic stress disorder, 67, 68
pregnancy stages
  first trimester, 8, 9, 31, 41, 50
  second trimester, 9
  third trimester, 9, 73
Pregnant Woman Support Act, 87–88
preimplantation genetic diagnosis, 91–92
premature birth, 9
Priests for Life, 78
pro-choice
  definition, 7, 17–18
  politics, 38
  positions, 19, 31, 42, 44–51, 53–59, 61, 67, 73, 81, 82, 83–84, 85, 86, 87, 89
  violence against, 77–78
progestin, 15
pro-life
  definition, 7, 17–19
  politics, 38, 40

  positions, 42, 54, 58–59, 61, 62–64, 66–75, 77–78, 81, 83–84, 85, 86, 92, 95
  protests, 5, 42, 46, 74–75, 77–78, 83
    graphic imagery, 18, 77
    Life Chain, 75
    Operation Rescue, 75, 77
    sidewalk counseling, 74–75
    truth trucks, 77
Public Conversations Project, 86
public opinion polls, 19, 59, 61, 81–82

Q

quickening, 9, 21, 24, 26, 27

R

rape, 7, 23, 30, 39, 40, 41, 48, 51, 54, 82, 83
Reagan, Ronald, 38, 94
Rehnquist, William, 34
religion, 21–24, 26, 38
reproductive health centers, 46
Republicans, 38, 86, 87, 92
Republican Majority for Choice, 38
Republicans for Choice, 38
Right to Life Act, 69
Roberts, John, 94
Roe, Jane, 32
Roe v. *Wade*, 7, 32, 34–35, 36, 37, 38, 39, 40, 42, 46, 64, 69, 94, 95
Roman Catholic Church, 24, 26, 75
RU-486, 10
rubella, 30–31
Russo, Nancy Felipe, 68

S

saline abortion, 14

Sanger, Alexander, 61
Sanger, Margaret, 61
Scalia, Antonin, 94
sex education, 46, 54–57, 70–71, 84
    abstinence–only, 55–57, 70–71, 84
    comprehensive, 54–56, 84
sexually transmitted disease (STDs), 46, 54, 55, 64, 70, 84, 87
Shays, Christopher, 86
Slepian, Barnett, 78
Social Security Act of 1996, 55
Souter, David, 94
sperm, 8, 12, 15, 51, 54, 91
Stachokus, John, 74
St. Antonius, 24
St. Augustine, 24
stem cells, 92
Stenberg v. Carhart, 36–37, 41
Stevens, John Paul, 94
Stop Deceptive Advertising for Women's Services Act, 59
suction aspiration, 13–14
Supreme Court, 32, 34, 35, 36, 37, 40, 41, 69, 74, 92, 93, 94, 95
surgical abortion, 10, 12–14
Swallow-Prior, Karen, 78

T
terrorism, 78
thalidomide, 31, 72
therapeutic abortion, 29–30

Thomas, Clarence, 94
Title X of the Public Health Service Act, 87
Torre-Bueno, Ava, 89
trigger laws, 37

U
Unborn Child Pain Awareness Act, 73
United States Congress, 7, 51, 53, 58, 59, 69, 86–87, 92–93
United States Constitution, 35, 37, 69

V
viability, 15, 34, 35, 36, 92
violence. See also protests.
    clinics, 42, 77–78, 83
    domestic, 48
    sexual, 48, 54

W
Wade, Henry, 32
waiting periods, 48–50, 51, 69, 70, 84
Waxman, Henry, 59
Webster v. Reproductive Health Services, 35
Weddington, Sarah, 32
White, Byron, 34
women's rights movement, 31
Wood, Deborah, 67
Wright, R. Frank, 73

Z
zygote, 8